GREAT ANARCHISTS

RUTH KINNA &
CLIFFORD HARPER

This edition first published in London, 2020 by Dog Section Press
and Active Distribution

ISBN 9781916036567

Originally published as a pamphlet series by Dog Section Press
and Active Distribution

ISSN 2631-3499-02

Printed by Calverts Ltd., a worker-owned cooperative

Graphic design by Matt Bonner • revoltdesign.org
Dog Section Press logo by Marco Bevilacqua

CONTENTS

INTRODUCTION

These short introductions delve into the anarchist canon to recover some of the distinctive ideas that historical anarchists advanced to address problems relevant to their circumstances. Although these contexts were special, many of the issues the anarchists wrestled with still plague our lives. Anarchists developed a body of writing about power, domination, injustice and exploitation, education, prisons and a lot more besides. Honing in on different facets of the anarchist canon is not just an interesting archaeological exercise. The persistence, development and adaptation of anarchist traditions depends on our surveying the historical landscape of ideas and drawing on the resources it contains. The theoretical toolbox that this small assortment of anarchists helped to construct is there to use, amend and adapt.

Educate! Agitate! Organise!

PETER KROPOTKIN

————

Kropotkin has many claims to greatness. An important conduit for the transmission of Russian revolutionary ideas into western Europe and a powerful propagandist for revolution in Russia in the decades leading up to 1917, he spent most of his life tirelessly promoting anarchism as a distinctive political philosophy and revolutionary practice. He played an instrumental role in two of the nineteenth-century movements' most influential papers, *Le Révolté* and *Freedom*, and was generally credited with being the founder of anarchist communism. This is inaccurate because Kropotkin was only one of a group of anarchists who advocated communism in the late 1870s and early 1880s. Still, he took a leading role in winning over comrades who identified as collectivists because they associated communism with rigid Jacobinism and he produced a large body of work explaining the libertarian alternative.

Kropotkin published in literary and scientific journals and newspapers as well as in the socialist and anarchist press. His work circulated in multiple translations and was read by revolutionaries across Europe, North America, Australia,

China and Japan. *The Conquest of Bread* was reputedly a favourite of Ricardo Flores Magon and helped him plot the contours of the Mexican Revolution. Kropotkin's defence of nihilistic ethics in *An Appeal to the Young* and his pithy critique of the wage system attracted anarchist as well as large non-anarchist audiences. Working closely with his friend Elisée Reclus, he advanced anarchy as an imaginable, attractive, attainable and sustainable condition. In *Fields, Factories and Workshops* he sketched a proposal for anarchist economic restructuring, based on the abandonment of the division between mental and manual labour, minute specialisation and the construction of self-supporting industrial villages.

Above all, Kropotkin's canonical status rests on the reception of *Mutual Aid*. His systematic analysis of co-operation forged a fruitful link between anarchy and anthropology and transformed a fuzzy idea of interdependence into a hallmark anarchist principle. It discredited yarns about human wickedness and ropey thought-experiments that centred on the state of nature and its miseries. Kropotkin argued that humans are perfectly capable of making their own rules and arrangements through their ordinary interactions and that the imposition of authority and the concentration of power permanently set social relations on a course of manipulation and lies. The book has left its mark on countless other anarchists including Murray Bookchin, Paul Goodman, Cindy Milstein, Brian Morris, Graham Purchase, Rudolf Rocker, Roel Van Duyn and Colin Ward.

Kropotkin didn't advance a unified, grand theory of anarchism but he did provide a consistent, compelling analysis of the state. Some of the early critiques he published in the *Newcastle Chronicle* were based on his examination of the harsh corruptions of Russian Tsarism. He later exposed the violence of the regime in *The Terror in Russia*. In *French and Russian Prisons* he used his extensive and intimate knowledge of incarceration to flesh out the disciplinary cultures that states fostered. In *Mutual Aid and The State: Its Historic Role* he presented a historical analysis of European exploitation, centralisation, bureaucratisation and militarisation. In an essay in *Freedom* he invoked the idea of 'Caesarism' to talk about the growing nationalistic and militaristic drift of European statism. And in *Wars and Capitalism* he discussed the instability, competitiveness and inherent aggression of the international state system.

Kropotkin is not without his detractors. His decision to back the Allied war effort against Germany in 1914 turned the greater part of the anarchist movement against him. As much as his promotion of anarchist science has excited his fans, it has also sullied his reputation in other quarters. Post-anarchists are wary of Kropotkin. However, his consistent, vehement rejection of Bolshevism and vanguard socialism, together with his practical approach to anarchist organising, have gone a long way to cement his standing as a potent advocate for anarchist communism.

KROPOTKIN WAS A COMMUNIST

When Kropotkin, Errico Malatesta, Carlo Cafiero and Elisée Reclus called on their comrades to embrace communism they worked hard to dispel the popular misconception that it was a system of government. It was just a principle of distribution. It meant distribution according to need as opposed to the collectivist principle of distribution according to work. Like collectivism, communism was intended to protect the commons and it entailed a commitment to egalitarianism. The chief difference was that communism meant accepting that people should not be rewarded for their individual efforts.

Kropotkin had three main reasons for recommending communism. First, he thought that individual reward systems encouraged exclusive rights to property ownership. Like Proudhon, he believed there was no moral basis for this. Everything we are and do and possess owes something to the efforts of others. Second, he believed that communist organisation had the advantage of simplicity. It was difficult to devise schemes to recompense individuals for their work or time or skill. The criteria were always contested and, once fixed, they were also inflexible. The results were invariably socially divisive, the mechanisms required to parcel out shares and payments were complex and cumbersome. Third, Kropotkin argued that anarchy would be forever unstable unless communism was adopted because any other system of distribution would eventually result in inequality, domination and the reinvention of the state. Kropotkin was generally critical of the philosopher Jean-Jacques Rousseau, but this was one argument he thought Rousseau had got right.

Kropotkin left the precise determination of needs open. And he also trusted local communities to work out how access to the commons should be organised. These judgements were always context specific and there could be no overarching plan.

Kropotkin's defence of communism got him into hot water with Spanish comrades who called for anarchy without adjectives, feeling that his labelling of anarchy was too prescriptive. It also put him at odds with anarchists who veered towards Benjamin Tucker, the editor of highly influential journal *Liberty*. Tucker argued that anarchists should respect the right of individuals to possess what they produced and/or the agreements that individuals entered into in order to secure those rights. Kropotkin thought that this form of anti-statism was unstable, even if it was well-intentioned. It encouraged the kind of self-interest and quest for competitive advantage that drove capitalist relations. It was also vulnerable to monopoly and the necessity to uphold individual rights augured the re-emergence of some form of state.

Kropotkin admitted that communism could be implemented in statist systems – one of the objections Tucker raised against him. He agreed with Tucker that Marxism was a form of state communism and that it followed the Jacobin model. But Kropotkin refused to accept that this was a necessary relationship. Unlike statist communism, anarchist communism was based on free agreement.

FREE AGREEMENT

Kropotkin talked about free agreement in *The Conquest of Bread* and in *Mutual Aid* but he gave one of his clearest and most succinct statements in his entry 'Anarchism' for the *Encyclopaedia Britannica*.

Kropotkin explained free agreement negatively by distinguishing it from contract. Free agreement described the kind of accord that liberal anti-statists typically dressed as contract, but it was at variance with it. The difference was threefold. First, contract was static. It had fixed provisions and assumed that contracting parties were equal in status and capability. In contrast, free agreement meant mutability and change and it was driven by the continual adjustment and re-adjustment of social forces that were unequal, complex and diverse. Whereas contracts were enforced with reference to their stipulations, free agreement ruled against the dictation of terms by one party on another and it was inconsistent with the idea of necessity.

The second difference was that free agreement disallowed consents secured through submission to law and those that depended on obedience to authority. Religious observance and marriage contracts typically fell into the first category.

Conscription and taxation were other examples because they were underwritten by constitutionally guaranteed rights to exclusive ownership. Turning to the repressive culture of contract, Kropotkin found the model in the prison system. Predicated on the idea of transgression, prison was designed to crush the will of prisoners, make them docile and break their inner strength. Prison deprived people of their liberty and stripped them of their capacity to live freely. People enjoyed more liberties on the outside but still inhabited worlds of regulated conformity, so still endured constraints on their freedom and suffered similar kinds of repression, albeit with less intensity.

In the third place, whereas law was based on fear, of one kind or another, free agreement was rooted in individual judgement. There was no servility in it because it allowed everyone to decide what they thought was right. Individuals were sovereign: they could restrict or expand their spheres of action and invoke their own moral standards in deciding how to live. Although the outcomes of their actions were never certain, free agreement released them from the threat of punishment, in this world or any other. In this respect, Kropotkin added a qualification to the idea of 'rules not rulers.' Rulers weren't ok but nor were rules if they were based on compliance with someone else's standards.

In sum: free agreement empowered individuals by guarding against economic domination and strict compliance with prevailing norms. Contract enslaved them by structuring economic inequality and enforcing obedience.

Like contract, free agreement operated in all social spheres: the family, the school, the workplace and in public institutions. Free agreement regulated inter-personal and inter-group relations. It was the glue that held anarchist networks of associations and more formal decentralised federations together. Because it was self-regulating, Kropotkin described it as a harmonious condition. By this he did not mean to suggest that it resulted in perfect freedom. It only provided the best protection against the entrenchment of domination and tyranny.

The lesson Kropotkin took from the historical sociology he plotted in *Mutual Aid* was that individuals were essentially social. They might not always behave well or even cultivate sociability. But humans were overwhelmingly found in groups and not in isolation, as conventional philosophy had it. So when individuals exercised their own will they inevitably came up against the traditions, habits, conventions and customs of the group. The mutability of free agreement was assured for as long as individuals were able to extend their liberties and push against the barriers to their freedom by challenging the forms of domination that groups institutionalised.

ANARCHISM AND ANTI-STATISM

One of the questions anarchists are routinely asked is to explain how their thinking differs from laissez-faire liberalism or anarcho-capitalism. Too often, the critique of the state is used to place anarchists alongside an endless parade of shock-jocks and politicians who call for the regulative powers of the state to be rolled back. As egalitarians, too, anarchists are put in the same box as right-libertarians who want to give free rein to capitalist market relations – some of them taking their lead from the writings of Benjamin Tucker. This is one reason why anarchism sometimes sends shivers down the backs of Marxists and social democrats.

Whether anarchists should deny the common ground they share with other anti-statists in order to avoid ideological confusion is a strategic question. Kropotkin's answer was 'no.' His view was that anarchists should go on the offensive. They should explain their positions, not give way to critics who were probably not interested in having sincere or open debates in the first place.

This was a perilous approach but Kropotkin decided that the potential gains outweighed the risks. Acknowledging the common concerns that anarchists and liberal anti-statists had about the increasing power and growing interventionism of states, he believed that he could demonstrate the consistency of anarchist-communism with individual self-expression and voluntary association while also demonstrating the failure of liberal anti-statists to deliver on anarchist egalitarianism. It was important to establish that anarchy was about individual free expression and the rejection of all forms of enslavement: patriarchal, colonial, clerical or racist. And it was possible to urge the refusal to conform and the courage to resist while drawing a line between the spirit of revolt, on the one hand, and aristocratic distain or naked egoism, on the other. The former was the dynamic for individual and collective direct action against injustice. The latter collapsed into a doctrine of might is right. Kropotkin could likewise agree that state regulation stifled individual initiative while spotlighting the flaws of those non-communist anarchist doctrines that grounded anarchism in the defence of rights. Anarchist communism fostered do-it-ourselves values without exposing social relations to the monopolistic logic of free market or neo-liberal injustice and the legal-statist protections that these doctrines demanded.

So Kropotkin combined a warm appreciation of the liberal anti-statist sociologist Herbert Spencer with a sharp condemnation of his defence of free-market economics. And he used this critique of Spencer to attack Tucker. Tucker, Kropotkin said, sailed too close to the liberal anti-statist wind and this made his anarchism flimsy.

In his entry on anarchism for the *Encyclopedia Britannica*, Kropotkin still included Tucker as a member of the anarchist family. He wasn't just being magnanimous or even straightforwardly strategic. He was committed to the principle of diversity and he saw the free flow of ideas as an essential ingredient for free agreement. Casting Tucker and his ilk outside the anarchist fold risked turning anarchism into a form of monasticism. Political parties subscribed to the same programmes and doctrines. Anarchists did not. As a revolutionary, Kropotkin struggled for anarchist communism. As an anarchist communist, he argued that there was no room for compromise with statist systems of domination, be they socialist, libertarian or republican. And as an anarchist he believed that the implementation of any ideal involved continuous struggle.

VOLTAIRINE DE CLEYRE

———

Voltairine de Cleyre was an essayist, educator, poet and advocate of anarchy without adjectives. Born in Michigan in 1866, she spent most of her adult life in Philadelphia surviving day-to-day teaching English. Working in a predominantly Jewish neighbourhood, she learned Yiddish well enough to translate articles from the local anarchist press into English. Her parents were abolitionists and free-thinkers who imprinted their fondness for the Enlightenment philosopher Voltaire on more than just her name. Voltairine's anarchism bore the hallmarks of their radicalism: the distrust of government and authority, sensitivity to injustice, anti-clericalism and confidence in the power of individual reason. Carried into her anarchism, these ideas ran through her critique of government as tyranny, her calls to revolt and her view that social transformation depended on constantly challenging accepted standards of justice, or what she called collective consciousness.

Voltairine's turn to anarchism was prompted by the trial of the Haymarket anarchists in 1887. This notoriously corrupt process had been triggered by a bombing at a labour demonstration in Chicago in 1886. Eight prominent anarchists were arrested in the police frenzy that followed. Perjury and prejudice resulted in the judicial killing of four of the defendants (George Engel, Adolph Fischer, Albert Parsons and Adolf Spies). A fifth, Louis Lingg, committed suicide while awaiting execution and a further three, Samuel Fielden, Oscar Neebe and Michael Schwab, were imprisoned until 1893 when the trial was reviewed and the sentences quashed.

Voltairine's initial horror on hearing the news about the explosion gave way to outrage at the state's repression of the anarchists. No attempt had been made to conceal the fact that the men were in the dock because they were anarchists, or that their actual involvement in the dynamiting was immaterial to the consideration of their guilt. At the very least, the flagrant trouncing of free speech begged questions about the fairness of the judicial process. Voltairine pushed further and concluded that the fraudulence of this trial exposed a systemic bias. Accepting the arguments that the Haymarket anarchists made in their lengthy, defiant defence speeches, she concluded that the constitution of the Republic was rotten, that its representatives had broken faith with the principles of the Revolution and that the continuity of the revolutionary tradition depended on the advancement of anarchy.

Voltairine's pamphlet *Anarchism and American Traditions* diagnosed the symptoms of America's decline: the limitless growth of government, the expansion of commerce and manufacturing and the spread of market values. The constitution had been designed to balance powers to protect the liberties of the people against the government. It had succeeded in concentrating power in the hands of financial and exploitative elites. It was supposed to preserve local independence but it had become a tool for the promotion of debt-fuelled subsistence economies and tax-funded government deficit-financing. The constitution was born from resistance to colonialism. It was now an instrument of empire. Americans had sworn to maintain their militias. Yet when government agreed the second amendment right to bear arms, leaving citizens free to pursue their grievances against each other, it also tooled itself up with a standing army and navy. Corruption was rife at every level of social life. The love of liberty had been traded for the pursuit of trippery. The new dream of the new world was material comfort, leisure and conspicuous consumption. Negligence was preferred to vigilance. Free speech, self-reliance and mutual support had gone out of the window. Instead of guarding their liberties, Americans had succumbed to a system of education that stupefied and brutalised. It was better equipped to turn unthinking patriots out of the classrooms than it was to foster reflective, active citizenship. Her European comrades argued similarly, and had she turned her gaze elsewhere she would have undoubtedly appreciated the resonances.

Voltairine's analysis of complicity makes for hard reading. Likewise her steadfast commitment to principle is difficult to emulate. Shot at point blank range three times by a former student in 1902, she not only refused to identify her attacker, thus scuppering the possibility of his prosecution, she also wrote a letter absolving him of his offence. But there's a lesson of empowerment in her critique of slavery and colonialism. It's based on direct action and the reclamation of rights.

SLAVERY AND COLONIALISM

The leading idea that Voltairine took from the Haymarket anarchists was that slavery had never been abolished. The prohibition on chattel slavery in 1863-65 in fact marked its transformation. This argument was not intended to downplay or devalue the history and experience of enslavement but to point out that emancipation had altered the character of domination while making sure that the principle of mastership was preserved. Freed slaves were no longer owned by masters. Yet liberation amounted to the freedom to join the ranks of wage slaves. Ex-slaves were still dependant on their former masters. This dependency was built into the law and it helped explain its evident distortions.

At the trial, the Chicago anarchists had focused on labour exploitation. Their argument was that wage slaves were compelled to compete for employment and authorised to enter into labour contracts that were trumpeted as free, but underpinned by structural inequality. Employers had the legal right to assert exclusive ownership over vast tracts of land, industrial plant and the profits derived from this. They were also at liberty to enforce these rights by violence. So when Chicago workers went on strike to press for the 8-hour day, employers paid armed security to shoot them. Leo Tolstoy put the same case, thinking about the 1861 Emancipation of the serfs in Russia as well as American abolition. He found the image for liberation in the practices of the Tartars of Crimea. Before they released prisoners from their shackles, they would slit the soles of their feet and press bristles into the wounds. This prevented escape while guaranteeing the supply of labour.

Voltairine took this argument in two other directions. On the one hand, she thought about the ways that slavery was perpetuated globally. On the other, she considered how slavery was felt differently in realms other than labour. The first informed her critique of colonisation. The second led her to advance an analysis of sexual domination.

The Mexican Revolution of 1910-11 crystallised her critique of colonial domination. Treating the revolution as a mobilisation against global economic domination she observed that repeated waves of settlers had exploited, imprisoned and massacred the indigenous populations. The main driver of this tyranny was the same as in the US: economic gain. At the point of the uprising, enormous swathes of Mexico were in the hands of a small number of families. Some holdings were the size of New Jersey, she observed. Having taken possession of the land these families were in a commanding position to force the local population to labour as slave-tenants. Voltairine called it plantation culture without chattel slavery.

The brutality of the Mexican enslavement highlighted another aspect of slavery: racism. Comparing the conquest of Mexico and the appropriation of the common lands to the Norman Invasion of England, Voltairine observed the sentiments that accompanied the Mexican government's appropriation of remaining common lands. The aim was to modernise by selling concessions to financiers and corporations, so attracting inward investment. It promised the systematic exploitation of natural resources and railways to facilitate it. It was a 'civilising mission' and it assumed that the indigenous people were backward – incapable of modernising by their own efforts and too stupid to see the benefits.

Voltairine's analysis of sex slavery was also rooted in an analysis of dependency. In this case, domination was explained by the dependence of men on women and the enslavement of women, seduced in one way or another by the arrangements that men made for their keep. Borrowing Proudhon's idea, she declared that women were property: slaves to men just as workers were enslaved to owners. Unequal pay, marriage laws, unpaid domestic labour, the presumption of women's intellectual incapability, paternity rights that granted ownership of children to fathers and awarded reproduction rights to husbands were some of the leading features of this regime.

The duty to protect, sanctified by the Church, provided the moral cover for this tyranny. It was suffocating and it operated as much in women's minds as it did through the cosseting institutions men created. Voltairine's conclusion was that domination would survive the abandonment of those institutions for as long as current behaviours were unaltered. In *They Who Marry Do Ill*, Voltairine admitted that marriage law was generally repressive; however, the tough message of the essay was that slavery was reinforced by monogamy and co-habitation, not merely by state or Church control of intimate relationships. Women stripped themselves of their capacity to meet their own basic needs independently of their menfolk by accepting the role of homemaker. This was not a call for abstinence, though Voltairine anticipated that the birth rate would fall once women released themselves from male domination. The collapse of close communion was a requirement for the constant innovation she associated with anarchy. Women had to live separately to be truly independent.

Women's enslavement was not merely economic, not merely political, not merely social or sexual. It was tied up with the regulation of human affections. Where domination reigned, love was a conservative force. Even in the most affectionate relationships, partners would stifle their better judgements to appease spouses and preserve the mundane friendships that passion bred. Turning love back into an emancipatory power meant loosening family bonds, celebrating fleeting romance, organising collective responsibility for childcare and fully recognising individual self-expression. Voltairine directed her remarks to other women but her views had implications for anyone who linked liberation to the extension of heterosexual rights and norms.

DIRECT ACTION AND RIGHTS

Voltairine's call for direct action followed from her analysis of the bankruptcy of the Republic. Law and government could not function as independent arbiters of justice because they were dependant on the exploitative capitalist systems they regulated. Nor could the existing systems be appropriated by the oppressed and redeployed for revolutionary purposes, no matter how lyrically conventional socialist philosophers waxed to the contrary. The only way individuals could combat slavery was to assert themselves as free beings by taking direct action.

Direct action was a principle not a tactic. The difference between suffrage campaigners and anarchists was that the former worked outside the frameworks of institutional politics for instrumental reasons. Anarchists were committed to direct action because they believed in acting for themselves. Direct action established their independence. This was Voltairine's theme in *The Gates of Freedom*. Direct action meant taking liberty not waiting for deliverance, propagandising by words and deeds and by "*being* what we teach." It had whatever content activists gave it and it also meant asserting rights.

For someone who disputed the benefits of the suffrage, this defence of rights seems odd. Yet Voltairine had a particular conception in mind. Rights were not one-off permissions or entitlements granted by authority. They were temporary measures of justice and their power derived from their general recognition. Rejecting the idea that there were any universal measures of right and wrong, justice and injustice, Voltairine nevertheless believed that it was possible to consider rights as mechanisms for social progression for as long as the demand challenged accepted practices and standards.

Demanding rights was inevitably disruptive. It compelled the enslaved to acknowledge their enslavement and expose the injustice of practices and behaviours that were generally believed to be natural, right and fair. Progress, Voltairine argued, was marked by the "transition from content to discontent, from satisfaction to pain" and "from unconsciousness to consciousness." Individual will and collective force both had a place in the process. Conflict was always likely because actions that directly threatened entrenched interests would create a backlash. The colonised should expect masters to deploy extraordinary force to quell their rebellions. Men would likewise be hurt, albeit in a different way, when women pressed their demands, though physical violence was common in this realm, too. And it would take time for everyone to adjust at every subsequent round of the struggle.

When Voltairine argued "they have rights who dare maintain them" she understood the enormity of the barriers that inhibited change. Slaves couldn't run with their feet chained together, cry when they were gagged, raise their hands above their heads when they had already been pinned to their sides. She was enraged when she was asked why women put up with their enslavement. "Will you tell me where they shall go and what they shall do?" In the days when the fugitive slave law compelled "men to catch their fellows more brutally than runaway dogs," chattel slaves had a fighting chance of making it to Canada. There was no such refuge for women. Wherever they were, they would have to dig their trenches and "win or die."

Voltairine maintained a strong belief that there was a tipping point for every injustice and that oppressed peoples would eventually find a way to strike out against their oppression. This is what she argued in her final poem, *Written in Red (To Our Living Dead In Mexico's Struggle)*. The Biblical myth of Daniel's warning to the tyrannous Belshazzar that his kingdom faced imminent destruction, captured her thought that liberty would tackle domination:

> Written in red their protest stands
> For the gods of the World to see;
> On the dooming wall their bodiless hands
> have blazoned "Upharsin," and flaring brands
> Illumine the message: "Seize the lands!
> Open the prisons and make men free!"

MICHAEL BAKUNIN

Bakunin has probably generated more trashy literature than any other anarchist. In Victorian penny-dreadfuls he appears by turns as an unstable fanatic and a pitiable fraud. In quite a lot of the subsequent scholarly writing he is at best a naive social dreamer, usually unhinged and unaware of his dictatorial tendencies, and at worst a manipulative, hypocritical schemer. Anarchists, of course, paint a different picture. Back in the day, Bakunin was feted as a champion of libertarian socialism and he is still celebrated as Marx's most redoubtable adversary. It was a complicated relationship: recognising Marx's genius as a social theorist, Bakunin judged him a serious but insincere revolutionary.

Bakunin's acolytes disagreed about the significance of his bust-up with Marx in the First International. Some of them argued that his critique showed that he was Marx's most reliable interpreter. Others thought that his rejection of Marx's programme for the International uncovered Marxism's fundamental theoretical flaws. However his admirers called it, the Bakunin-Marx clash had a massive organisational impact and the ripples are still felt today. The revolutionaries who wanted to distance themselves from the centralising, programmatic policy changes that Marx engineered in the International identified Bakunin as the personification of anti-authoritarian socialism or anarchism. Numbering Kropotkin, Malatesta and Reclus among his adherents, he became the towering figure of European anarchism in the late nineteenth century.

Quite a lot of ink has been spilt on Bakunin's shaky judgments, particularly his relationship with Sergei Nechaev. There's a lot to question and even to dislike in his writing, notably his cultural stereotyping and anti-Semitism. Both are evident in his critique of Marx. But having survived two death-sentences and brutal treatment at the hands of the Russian state, Bakunin remained active in the nascent international anarchist movement and managed to produce some of the most exhilarating, inspiring prose in the anarchist back-catalogue.

A-HISTORICAL MATERIALISM

Bakunin was an anti-utopian thinker in the sense that he rejected philosophical approaches to politics that relied on the deployment of pure abstract concepts to promote political goals. Naturally it was possible to conceptualise justice and right and liberty and it was empowering to imagine alternative realities; however, the use of philosophy to promote idealised social systems was wrong-headed because it typically airbrushed real inequalities and injustices from view and too often resulted in a type of ideological practice that legitimised arbitrary power and oppression. Moreover, the whole exercise placed judgments about political goals and values in the hands of rarefied elites. However clever these people were – and that was by no means guaranteed – Bakunin believed that removing the power of evaluation from ordinary people was wrong. The end result was the replacement of self-government with government.

Bakunin's alternative was based on the view that material conditions gave meaning to ideas of justice, right and liberty. Once this was understood, it was possible to see that the advancement of any fixed ideal was distorting. History taught that the exercise had repeatedly forced people to adopt behaviours that benefitted those who commanded the most resources: the richest, the most heavily armed, those who garnered the most respect, the silver-tongued and persuasive, the boldest, egotistically super-confident and often, sadly, the most ruthless. At the same time, the re-alignment of political philosophy to sociology revealed that the historical experience of injustice, arbitrary rule and repression concealed other sets of values and ideas. It was liberating to discover that social life generated its own orders and that the elaborate artifices that had been invented to perfect human life were redundant. Bakunin described the insight as science. Likewise he called the spontaneous patterning of social life that science detected 'natural' because it was structured by norms, values and ideals that emerged from everyday human interactions.

The critique of elitism that Bakunin took from his materialist worldview provided the impetus for social transformation. Anarchy was about restoring natural order by re-prioritising the material over the ideal. There was no pristine Lost World of Atlantis to recover. Instead the process involved the destruction of utopian idealism and the creative reconstruction of social life by the least powerful and the oppressed. Promoting the news that the uneducated, unrefined rabble was capable of organising collective actions to advance conceptions of justice, right and liberty gleaned from the historical experience of their negation was the lifeblood of anarchist change.

Though not lacking an interest in history, Bakunin was unimpressed with philosophical schema designed to show its direction of travel. Having freed himself from the lure of German metaphysics in the 1840s, soon after he first met Marx, he set about turning Hegel, the metaphysician of metaphysicians, on his head. Marx had set out to do the same but in Bakunin's book he mistakenly retained Hegel's notion that history contained a logic. Like his teacher, Marx believed that history pointed towards the expansion of the realm of freedom. Marx replaced Hegel's idealist concept of Reason with a materialist reading of productive force. This elicited a critique of capitalism that Bakunin broadly endorsed and it injected a materialist component into a utopian-idealist worldview. Yet it left Hegel firmly on his feet:

Marx's certainty that capitalism provided the preconditions for socialism, that the victory of the proletariat was assured and that temporary dictatorship needn't be dictatorial were all explained by this reading of history.

Bakunin removed the motive force from history altogether. This didn't mean that social change was reduced to a matter of will. There was always a context for struggle. The point was that there was no dynamic other than action, and contingency was all.

POLITICAL THEOLOGY

As a materialist, Bakunin was also an atheist. Famously calling for God's abolition he argued that moral sense was rooted in varying and transient social practices, not in the universal or the Divine. This dismissal of God didn't stop Bakunin from describing himself as a man of faith. He had faith in science insofar as it elevated earthly life over otherworldly existence and he had faith in the future, even after the crushing of the Paris Commune in 1871. In fact the example of the Commune fired his irreverent belief that humans were actively engaged in struggles to release themselves from pacifying political theology.

Political theology was not identical to religion, though it was related to it. Religions were belief systems that humans invented and alienated from themselves, thus creating benchmarks to assess their own behaviours. In its purest form, political theology was the view that humanity was base, sinful and corrupt and that all that was beautiful, worthy and pure depended on revelation and obedience to God's self-appointed representatives. The story of Eden and the Fall provided the model, as it was conventionally told as a tale of wrong-doing, expulsion and punishment with the hope of redemption conditional on supplication.

Reinforced in art and literature, political theology underpinned political idealism and justified hierarchy and authority. It encapsulated the view that discipline and mastership made social life possible, so legitimising structural domination. Patriarchy was one of its symptoms. At the end of *Statism and Anarchy*, Bakunin tore into romantic cults of the Russian peasantry by launching an unrelenting attack on the traditional family. The good man – the father, the husband, the elder brother – was in fact a weasely tyrant. Habituated to obedience he was subservient to the men of the village, a slave to the Tsar, and he measured his freedom by enjoying unlimited despotism at home.

If patriarchy was a result of the cultural diffusion of political theology, statism was the upshot of its integration into philosophy. The relationship to absolutism had been made obvious by the great eighteenth-century revolutions but, as far as Bakunin was concerned, republicanism and Jacobin communism were still enmeshed in it. It was entirely possible for committed, honest revolutionaries to espouse emancipatory causes while simultaneously proposing programmes that simply changed the terms of enslavement.

Jean-Jacques Rousseau was a case in point. Having advanced a brilliant critique of private property and the liberal social contract, he proposed a form of association that was every bit as despotic, obliging each to alienate themselves and their property to the state in the name of the common good and moral freedom. Anarchy was the counter and Bakunin reworked the story of Genesis to drive the point home. In his telling, Eve's decision to eat the apple was an act of wilful disobedience and the flight from Eden was a conscious bid for liberation from domination.

Looking at the European political landscape, Bakunin observed that political theology had been effectively instrumentalised by Machiavellian diplomats and politicians: Mouravieff in Russia, Metternich in Austria, Cavour in Italy, Bismarck in Germany, Palmerston in Britain and Louis Napoleon in France. Their game was to exploit the ideological pull of political theology in order to advance the interests of the state. For as long as they played along, clerics were tolerated in the domestic realm, but statesmen now relied on finance capital not sacrament to sanction their rule. European politics was shaped by the machinations of these great men of history but the operation of the international state system was underwritten by capitalist monopoly.

Understanding capitalism as an independent force in European affairs, Bakunin argued that the systematic exploitation of labour, quickened by industrialisation and driven by selfish, bourgeois commercial interests, constituted a distinctive kind of oppression. Nonetheless, capitalist monopoly was always implicated with the state and steadily increasing concentrations of capital helped explain processes of centralisation, bureaucratisation and militarisation. These shifts were driven by corporate interests. Bakunin's wager, then, was that the struggle against tyranny and state oppression was necessarily a struggle against capitalism. Yet class struggle was hidebound for as long as political theology held sway. The use of state institutions to regulate, control or abolish capitalism would only succeed in redirecting the flow of economic power into new channels of authority. Moreover, it would do nothing to eradicate the persistent tyrannies embedded in social relations.

FREEDOM STRUGGLES

Bakunin declared himself a fanatical lover of liberty who brooked no limits on freedom, and a realist who recognised that individual action was always constrained. People couldn't actually do exactly what they liked, at least not all the time. The apparent contradiction is explained by the two different ideas of liberty Bakunin stitched together. One was linked to domination and the other was associated with equal capability. Non-domination meant being regarded as a moral equal and following one's own rules. Equal capability meant being able to enjoy the same level of well-being as everyone else. Bakunin's example of Bluebeard's wife illustrates the difference. She was dominated but had greater capability than other women. With a house full of riches at her disposal, she had free reign of the house only for as long as she observed Bluebeard's command to stay out of his underground chamber: transgression spelt death.

In the capitalist state these types of unfreedom usually went hand in hand. Rural and industrial workers were treated as inferior to the educated bourgeoisie and made to obey rules that they had no part in making; because the rules were formulated to benefit the owners and employers, they were also deprived of education and crushed by forced labour, hunger and poverty. In terms of their capability they were also less free than their masters; however, the unfreedoms of the capitalist state were not always evenly balanced. In patriarchy, women experienced domination more keenly than men.

Bakunin pushed the argument in the context of patriotism, national liberation and colonial domination – the dynamic forces of his age. He made two crucial distinctions. The first was between instinctive and political patriotism and the second was between nationality and nationalism. Instinctive patriotism was the sense of exclusive solidarity. It arose between people who lived in the same area and shared common habits and ways of life. Bakunin associated it with a hatred of difference but reserved his sternest strictures for political patriotism, the cultivation of aggressive xenophobia, typically bolstered by religious patriotism or the worship of an exclusive deity. Likewise, nationality was 'a fact' made manifest in the existence of local cultural practices, moral norms and linguistic diversity. Nationalism expressed certainty in the virtue and superiority of these particular traits.

Since the end of the Napoleonic wars, these social phenomena had intersected with each other in complex ways. On the one hand, instinctive patriotism had often militated against state formation. For example, relatively isolated communities in southern Italy had resisted the republican statist drive towards national unification, preferring local solidarity. On the other hand, politicians had also politicised instinctive patriotic sentiments to whip up aggressively nationalistic campaigns.

In the context of the rise of the European state, it was often difficult to tease out the political dynamics of social movements. Appreciating the complexity, Bakunin maintained that anarchy pointed towards the rejection of patriotism and towards internationalism. His vision was of a borderless world based on the extension of solidarity across localities and the recognition of the equal worth of local practices and diversity. Decentralised federalism provided the organisational framework, just as Proudhon had argued. In the meantime, Bakunin argued that national liberation struggles were often directed against domination and that they contained a socialistic element. European history indicated that they were easily hijacked by bourgeois capitalists and unscrupulous politicians. But the success of reactionary movements was guaranteed for as long as revolutionaries stood on the sidelines and left partisans to fight their own battles. The revolutionary alternative was to stand in solidarity and excavate the universal perspective against national domination, against capitalism, and for anarchist freedom.

LOUISE MICHEL

———

Educator, poet, dramatist, novelist, movement historian, orator and agitator Louise Michel rose to prominence during the Paris Commune (1870-71) and acquired a commanding public profile in the last decades of the nineteenth century. Michel was one of some 4,500 Communards deported to New Caledonia in 1872. When she was amnestied in 1880, an estimated 10,000-strong crowd gathered to greet her at Paris' St. Lazare station. Another 50,000 turned out in 1905 for her funeral. Michael Schaack's 1889 highly prejudicial history of anarchism correctly identified her as one of the leading lights of what he referred to darkly as the Red Internationale. Max Nettlau's more astute observation was that Michel's prestige was so immense that her mere presence at a meeting was enough to guarantee a large and enthusiastic audience.

Working as a teacher during the September 1870 siege of Paris, Michel organised a soup kitchen for her pupils before piloting the Montmartre Vigilance committees. These allocated work, received and distributed donations, arranged home visits to care for the sick, the elderly and the poor. She participated in the March 1871 actions that thwarted the Versailles government's attempts to disarm Paris and stood with the battalions at Montmartre in the Commune's final hours. Her surrender, prompted by the threat of her beloved mother's execution, resulted in her trial and deportation to New Caledonia.

Disappointment doesn't quite cover what Michel experienced when she witnessed the ferocious retribution the French government exacted on tens of thousands of Communards in the Bloody Week of May 1871, but she turned to anarchism convinced of the bankruptcy of republicanism. Prior to this she'd distinguished herself as a critic of Napoleon III, encouraged by the writer Victor Hugo, one of the Emperor's most taxing opponents. Not surprisingly given her involvement in the Union des Femmes, an organisation that united hundreds of militant women in the defence of Paris, she was rediscovered in the 1970s as an early and ardent feminist. Her nickname the Red Virgin has since sparked reflections on her sexuality. Internationalism was a persistent theme in her writing. Audacity was another. Her poem *Black Marseillaise* (1865) calls on the people to stop sleeping, stand up, and be "strong and great" – it's "the reluctant man that betrays tomorrow." In 1880 she endorsed Emile Gautier's Anarchist Manifesto. It decried capitalism, private property and government tyranny, chiming with her general view that power monopolised is evil. The last line called for bread for all, work for all, independence, and justice; it also demanded knowledge for all. This commitment to education was another thick seam in her politics, and one that she approached as a keen practitioner.

KNOWLEDGE, VIRTUE AND SCIENCE

Michel taught throughout her life, first in villages of the Haute-Marne close to her family home and then in Paris. She spent nine years in a day-school in Montmartre before buying her own establishment in 1865. In New Caledonia, she ran classes for the children of the indigenous people, the Kanaks. In 1890, when she left France for London, she launched the International Socialist School in Fitzrovia. Her methods were always innovative and usually regarded as subversive. Her habit of taking pupils outside to learn about natural science tipped the parents of her charges in Haute-Marne over the edge.

Michel understood education as a process of cultivation. It had two aspects: knowledge acquisition and the cultivation of the mind was one, the second centred on the development of virtue.

In bourgeois society, these aspects had been packaged to conflate the cultivation of virtue with technical prowess. This in turn was associated with a narrow programme of book-learning. The result was that instruction was characterised by discipline rather than discovery, and that the ability to regurgitate the findings of established scholars was revered as a sign of superiority. Anyone excluded from education – which was most of the population – was automatically deemed both stupid and brutish. Similarly, knowledge acquired from outside the prescribed curriculum was dismissed as unfounded and uncivilised.

Michel was not averse to book-learning. Nor was she disdainful of scholarship. She immersed herself in libraries, spent most of her earnings on books, and marvelled at her uncle's historical erudition. But her own education owed as much to her familiarity with the local landscapes, observation, and experimentation as it did to conventional reading, and she learned equally from stories, myths and legends as she did from the insights of the eminent. Education was about stimulating the imagination as well as absorbing facts. Michel habitually used drama and music to inspire her own pupils. When she settled in New Caledonia she had no difficulty appreciating the role that legend played in indigenous culture or in understanding the qualities that these tales helped nourish in the Kanak people. Mastering enough of the local language to educate herself, she studied their customs, music and oral traditions, noting the similarities with Scandinavian and European folk traditions and reporting the results to her European friends. The Kanaks were not civilised, as the French bourgeoisie styled themselves, and they lacked the technical ability that the colonisers possessed. So when they rebelled against their white masters in 1878, they were quickly mown down by superior weaponry. Almost alone in supporting the Kanak insurrection, Michel took the view that the rebels were the more cultured, because they lacked French manners.

Science properly linked knowledge acquisition and virtue. For Michel, science was a tool of empowerment and cultural improvement. Contentiously describing New Caledonia as the 'stone-age,' she imagined how advanced knowledge could be applied to alleviate suffering and hardship. Yet noticing at the same time that abominable forms of exploitation existed in the non-human as well as the human realm, Michel also argued that the potential for science to shape nature ethically depended on the adoption of particular approaches and methods.

Science relied on the acknowledgment of fallibility, the courage to challenge received wisdom, and the ability to harness talents in combined effort. Using status to shut down inquiry, dismissing new hypotheses by appealing to established truths, and rejecting new practices merely because they conflicted with existing norms were all deeply unscientific practices. Similarly, science could only be advanced by ethical methods. Michel therefore demanded the abandonment of animal experiments, convinced that use of cruel or exploitative methods fatally undermined the prospects of making any genuinely scientific advances. There was an integral relationship between ends and means.

WOMEN, EDUCATION AND TRANSFORMATION

Aware that rural workers of the Haute-Marne were largely excluded from education, Michel understood the class barriers to science at an early age. Yet it was the injustice and power inequalities that affected women that really exercised her as an anarchist. The idea that ordinary people had to go hungry at some point in the year, believing it was impossible to produce enough food to go around, was false knowledge; however, the most pernicious bogus science was reserved for women. She noticed that her own work was only considered interesting when she published under a male pseudonym and that she was ridiculed for experimenting with plant vaccines in New Caledonia because she was a mere woman-amateur. She saw too that special programmes of learning delivered to girls were designed to reinforce gendered hierarchy. No wonder that men were content to keep women in childlike states, convincing themselves that their own courage was necessitated by women's cowardice. Declaring the proletarian a slave, Michel noted that the wife of the proletarian was still more enslaved. And the same power relations prevailed in New Caledonia as in France. The word used by indigenous people for woman was *nemo*, meaning 'nothing.' Although Michel played on the idea when she endorsed the bravery of the Russian nihilist women who struck at the heart of tyranny by despatching their rulers, she believed that the term expressed a universal patriarchal sentiment.

Michel's observations complicated her calls for science to be re-grounded in the common sense of the people. While this was a good rule of thumb, she recognised that elites were not alone in lacking virtue. Too many people were habituated to the prejudices disseminated by false science. Under no illusion about the depth of popular ignorance, she despaired when she saw a Paris crowd gather in 1862 to revel in the republican Jules Miot's imprisonment. This was the same crowd that rallied for public executions, and its members could scarce be found when bodies were needed to rip up paving stones and build barricades. It was no more 'the people' than the Marseillaise was the anthem of the revolution once it had been appropriated by the Third Republic. For Michel 'the people' was a dynamic concept not a constituency. It was forged through revolutionary action not by mobilising opposition to random enemies of the republic. Even when it emerged, as it did in the defence of Paris, it was imperfect. Michel noted that her male comrades made encouraging sounds about women's organising but too often paid lip-service to the rights of women. Proudhon's conservatism cast a long shadow over the French revolutionary movement.

There was always room for more scientific education and Michel's view was that women would spearhead the next advances. Experience taught her that women were braver than men, less fainthearted and more able to accept necessity. Men advertised their importance by causing a lot of brouhaha: women went about their business quietly, but actually made the important decisions. Unlike men, they were capable of acting without hate, without anger and without pity. Noting that anarchy was often fostered by discipline, Michel argued that women were similarly spurred on by the villainy perpetrated against them: "We jeer at the incredible sight of big-shots, cheap punks, hoods, old men, young men, scoundrels – all turned into idiots by accepting as truth a whole heap of nonsensical ideas which have dominated the thinking of the human race. We jeer at the sight of those male creatures judging women's intellects by weighing the brains of women in their dirty paws."

SOCIAL TRANSFORMATION

The premise underpinning Michel's educational practice was that everyone was educable. Her response to the Breton sharp-shooters who fired on demonstrators standing outside the Hôtel de Ville in January 1871 was that they were misguided but not beyond instruction. One day they would be able to see that they had acted from a misplaced sense of duty and they would take up her cause. The question she asked herself was how to close the gap between infallible false knowledge and fallible true science.

Michel had no pat answers and proposed continual propaganda. This of course included insurrection but also writing, lecturing, orchestrating strikes and even fly-posting police officers' coats when the wall space ran out. Michel was not averse to targeted assassination either. Hugo had taught her the virtue of republican violence. Taking the lesson into her anarchism, she refused to condemn the so-called propagandists by the deed whose acts shocked the bourgeois world in the 1890s. She further argued that tyrannicide was effective in absolutist and oligarchic regimes and that, ethically, the nihilists were right to argue that it was better to kill one person than allow mass slaughter.

Making some room for consequential reasoning in anarchist practice, Michel was torn on the question of electioneering. On the one hand she argued that illegal 'dead' candidacies – those that inevitably resulted in the disbarring of successful candidates – had some propaganda value. She therefore allowed her name to go forward on a candidate list for the 1881 general election because women were prohibited from voting or serving as representatives. The symbolic action asserted a rightful demand for equality. On the other hand she admitted that the promotion of dead candidacies could be misconstrued. One possibility was that the gesture could be mistaken as a commitment to a sectional cause. Observers might wrongly conclude that Michel prioritised the equality of women over the advancement of human emancipation by women's revolutionary action. The other possibility was that her participation in the process would legitimise the electoral process by instigating demands for its reform. Firmly convinced that electioneering was pointless, she withdrew her candidacy.

Michel's reflections on this issue highlighted another aspect of her approach to education. This touched on her personal sense of virtue and the integrity of revolutionary memory. Emerging from the Commune with her hopes of change intact, Michel also revised down her estimations of likely short-term gains. Taking a longer view, she concluded that the construction of the Commune's history was part of the revolutionary struggle. Only too aware that she was the subject of grotesque press misreporting and that her reputed ugliness was part and parcel of the Commune's demonisation, she used every platform at her disposal to promote the beauty of revolutionary ideas. Her refusal to acknowledge court authority, her defiant acknowledgment of her responsibility for inciting insurrection, and her demand that the judges execute her were all acts of self-curation. Believing that revolutionaries were bullets adapted to struggle, Michel wanted it known that she was unapologetic and forever wedded to revolutionary transformation. She adopted the same stance in 1883, when accused of riot and looting. Was she moved by the charges? No, absolutely indifferent. She only challenged the evidence "for the sake of the honour of the Revolution." She fired back at the prosecutor: "I have never prostrated myself in front of anyone, and I have never asked for mercy. You can say anything you want to about us, you can sentence us to prison, but I do not want you to dishonour us."

OSCAR WILDE

***

Scholar, poet, playwright, socialite and wit, Wilde is one of those magnetic figures that everyone now seems to want to claim a piece of. His literary genius accounts for some of the competition. But the vindictiveness of the reaction to his public disgrace as a "posing sodomite" is at least as significant for his story. Wilde endured two years of hard labour after his libel action against the Marquis of Queensbury, father of his lover Lord Alfred Douglas, collapsed. When the jury at his first trial failed to reach a verdict the Crown felt compelled to retry the case: he received the maximum sentence for 'gross indecency.' Wilde was the cultural superstar of his age and he was dropped like a stone. His name was removed from theatre hoardings, performances of his plays ceased; friends disappeared and the institutions that had once gloried in their association with him moved quickly to erase his memory. Wilde's illustrious school in Enniskillen – the so-called Eton of Ireland – scratched his name from the honours board that boasted his scholarship to Trinity College, Dublin – later restoring it when Wilde was rehabilitated. The ferocity of the public outrage explains why liberals, libertarians of all stripes, and especially gay rights campaigners are now eager to declare him as their own.

Can anarchists also lay claim to Wilde? *The Soul of Man Under Socialism*, the essay he published in 1891, usually puts him in the anarchist frame, typically as a kind of individualist. As the book makes clear, the individualism Wilde had in mind was defined by art. This was the "most intense mode" of individualism the world had ever known.

Wilde's defence of art explained why, taking aim at orthodox Marxist social democracy, he rejected authoritarian and "industrial-barrack socialism." It also explained why he despaired of common-sense reformist socialism: the socialism of the Fabians and other democratic do-gooders. This was practical, dull, unadventurous and unambitious. Its proposals were conceivable in conditions that were objectionable and which should be rejected as "wrong and foolish." It charted a map of the world that did not include utopia and so it was "not worth even glancing at." Art was equally at the heart of Wilde's reformulation of Henry David Thoreau's observation "that government is best which governs least." Wilde's version was: "the form of government that is most suitable to the artist is no government at all." Finally, Wilde's conception of art as individualism contextualised his depiction of Kropotkin as the "beautiful White Christ." The apparently flowery language Wilde used in *De Profundis*, the letter he wrote in 1897 just before his release, builds on the interpretation of Christ's message that he presents in *The Soul of Man*. This was "Be thyself." That Kropotkin had experienced the hardships and humiliations of prison was significant for Wilde, but the fulsome praise he heaped on Kropotkin reflected his view that Kropotkin had followed Christ's teaching precisely. Having had the option of keeping his head down and enjoying his privilege, Kropotkin decided that he could not live contentedly in conditions that denied the soul's development. Indeed, Kropotkin was the nihilist who rejected "all authority because he knows authority to be evil, and welcomes all pain, because through that he realises his personality." Throwing in his lot with the anarchists, Kropotkin became the "real Christian" – artist and individualist.

Should anarchists claim Wilde? Anarchists should surely reserve a place for him in the pantheon of Great Anarchists, but perhaps should not expect him to rush to fill it. Wilde never identified as anarchist and he dodged all the ideological markers that were beginning to be applied in the late nineteenth century. Wilde's first play, *Vera; or the Nihilist*, was a disaster, closing in New York only a week after it opened, and he quickly disowned it. Yet for all his embarrassment about its literary merits, his choice of topic gave a clue to the tenor of his thinking. He described himself as a "born antinomian" – someone who rejects moral law and obligation on the basis of faith. He was "made for exceptions, not for laws." His social theory bore the imprint of William Morris' socialism. The ethos of the arts and crafts movement was stamped all over the lectures he delivered in North America in the 1880s, just before his rise to fame, and it is detectable in *The Soul of Man*, too. Yet Wilde directed his invective against social compliance rather than capitalism per se. Moreover, *The Soul of Man* had little of the romance of Morris' *News From Nowhere*, published the year before. Wilde injected Morris' love of nature and decorative art with a more flamboyant, darker aesthetic. His friend and literary executor Robert Ross spotted an affinity with Nietzsche. In the twentieth century the art-historian Herbert Read reworked this striking amalgamation, albeit to very different effect. Art and creativity were central to both but whereas Read recruited art principally to the service of education, Wilde pursued it to find a path to deliverance.

AGAINST DEMOCRACY

Unexcited by the promise of the Gettysburg Address, Wilde rewrote Abraham Lincoln's epigram about democracy as "the bludgeoning of the people by the people for the people." He was opposed to democracy for two reasons. First, democracy was a form of government and like other forms it was a mechanism for the exercise of authority. In contrast to oligarchy, which was "unjust to the many," or ocholcracy (mob rule), which was "unjust to the few," democracy was most like despotism: "unjust to everybody, including the despot." It replicated the "sceptre of the

Prince" and the "triple tiara of the Pope." Yet in contrast to despotism, it was not obviously unjust. On the contrary, democracy was the kindest form of government and it used carrots rather than sticks to bring people to heel. This was the peoples' opiate – not religion, as Marx had it – because it rendered the routine cruelty and brutality of government acceptable, thereby dampening opposition to tyranny.

Wilde's second objection to democracy was that it left class divisions between rich and poor intact. These were rooted in property ownership. Wilde argued that property imposed burdens on the rich and poor alike, channelling the energies of the owners to the preservation of the prestige and status that property conferred and reducing non-owners to poverty and starvation. The effect was the same in both cases: the worship of property "crushed true individualism" and made "gain not growth its aim." Wilde admitted that the rich were more able to realise individualism than the poor. Byron, Shelley, Victor Hugo, Baudelaire all fell into this category. But he nonetheless believed that property compromised art: none of these writers was able to achieve what they might otherwise have accomplished in a propertyless regime. Likewise, taking issue with the scholars who celebrated the great men of history, Wilde denied that Caesar or the emperor-philosopher Marcus Aurelius had perfected themselves. A perfect life could only be lived in perfect conditions, where one was not "wounded, or worried or maimed, or in danger." Property made this impossible.

Democracy was toothless against property because class tensions reinforced the principle of ownership. Property owners lived in perpetual fear that a sudden change in economic fortunes would strip them of all their possessions and the rights that came with them, but never dreamed of giving up their assets for the sake of serenity. The poor, too, struggled to maintain property. If they were keen to alleviate the worst effects of maldistribution, their aspiration was to be rich and possess the things property laws denied them. Indeed, poverty had so degraded the poor that most were unable to understand that property was the cause of their suffering. Wilde commented that starved peasants had happily died for "the hideous cause of feudalism" during the French revolution. Likewise he believed that too many of the poor had absorbed the language of virtue, thrift and charity to utilise democracy as a tool for property's abolition.

Democracy levelled out access to rights and removed the exclusive liberties and powers that property owners enjoyed: its promise was to stabilise the power relations and hierarchies of knowledge that property underpinned. In authority the people were politically disempowered but culturally supreme. Having once bemoaned the arbitrary power of the despot, they now revelled in their capacity to determine what was right, good, just, virtuous and beautiful, and impose these standards uniformly. Eagerly punishing waywardness and rejoicing in their obedience to the rules and conventions they introduced, the people had become oblivious to their own degeneration. Democrats went through life as automatons, "thinking other people's thoughts, living by other people's standards, wearing practically… other people's second hand clothes, and never being themselves for a single moment." If by some fluke they appreciated the uncommon art of an individual, they usually absorbed it without any reflection on the oppression they exercised. The people were priests without souls.

By altering the basis of authority and retaining class divisions, democracy summoned two appalling monsters into being: public opinion and popular taste. These were in fact creatures of the deeply conservative elite in which journalists and critics prevailed. Wilde was horrified by their dogmatism and banality. Journalists "invite the public to discuss an incident, to exercise authority in the matter, to give their views… to carry them into action, to dictate to the man upon all other points, to dictate to his party, to dictate to his country… to make themselves ridiculous, offensive, and harmful." They "supply the public with what the public wants" and "compete with other journalists in making that supply as full and satisfying to the gross popular appetite as possible." Critics exacerbated the problem by acting as brakes on innovation and experiment. They assessed art by the standards of the past to maintain the status quo. Wilde called the past "what man should not have been" and the present "what man ought not to be." Democracy structured both long into the future and was anathema to art and true individualism.

ART ACTIVISM

Wilde recommended disobedience – "man's original virtue" – as the cure for democracy. Physical force was one aspect of this art, probably the best form available to the impoverished. Just as charity reduced the have-nots, rebellion ennobled them. An "ungrateful, unthrifty, discontented" poor man had real personality. Wilde admitted it was safer to beg than to steal but believed it was "finer to take than to beg." His view dovetailed with Emma Goldman's recommendation: "Ask for work. If they don't give you work, ask for bread. If they do not give you work or bread, then take bread." Identifying individualism with the spirit of revolt and fearful that democracy would smother it, he also called for agitators to "sow the seeds of discontent" amongst the poor. Wilde rejected the view that force signalled a failure of reason. Violent revolution made "the public grand and splendid for a moment." It had also "solved entirely" some of "most important problems of the last few centuries," notably "the continuance of personal government in England" and "the feudalism of France." Returning to the theme of press freedom and justice, he commented that it was "a fatal day when the public discovered that the pen is mightier than the paving stone, and can be made as offensive as the brickbat."

Refusing to bow to public opinion was his preferred strategy. This form of disobedience was not rebellious or deliberately transgressive, for that gave too much ground to tyranny. Byron had battled too long with "stupidity and hypocrisy and Philistinism." In Shelley, too, the "note of rebellion" was too strong. In terms of professional practice, the non-compliant artist "selects his own subject, and treats it as he chooses." The insubordination was the refusal to draw inspiration from the past in order to make art intelligible, popular or marketable. Thus the individualist created something that had never been. In a broader sense, Wilde's view was that artists perfected personality through self-reflection, just as Christ had done. In this sense, too, individualism was about self-expression and creation and behaving as one willed, whether or not others approved. But above all, it was about finding peace with oneself. Jesus said: "You have a wonderful personality. Develop it. Be yourself. Don't imagine that our perfection lies in accumulating or possessing external things... Ordinary riches can be stolen from a man. Real riches cannot."

Wilde denied that the individualism he cherished was selfish or egotistical. Selfishness "is not living as one wishes to live, it is asking others to live as one wishes to live." Artists were unselfish because they let everyone follow their own paths. They had no desire to impose on others: this was egotistical. He also denied that art was self-sacrificing. Self-sacrifice was about duty. Art was about inclination and voluntarism. It admitted no compulsion; however, individualism involved pain and demanded resilience. Inevitably, individualists would confront hatred, fear and ignorance. Wilde cautioned the true personality not to fight but suffer and find sympathy in suffering. The real Christ was "maimed and marred." He was the tortured, sombre soul depicted in medieval art, not the beautiful composed figure that featured in Renaissance pastels. Artists would find their souls living "intensely, fully, perfectly," tolerating pain as "provisional and a protest." The present seemed bleak but the prospects for art were good. Wilde looked forward to joyful individualism in socialism. Refusing all laws and authority except its own, it would be "freer, far finer, and far more intensified than it is now."

OSCAR WILDE

MAX STIRNER

————

Born Johann Kaspar Schmidt in Beyreuth in 1806, Stirner is one of the most controversial anarchists, by turns celebrated as the seminal anarchist theorist and marginalised as a political philosopher only tangentially related to the anarchist movement. The nineteenth-century commentator E.V. Zenker billed Stirner as the German Proudhon, one of the movement's two intellectual forerunners; Paul Eltzbacher listed him as one of the seven exponents of anarchist philosophy. His reputation has fared less well over time and recently anarchist-communists have rejected him from anarchism's history.

Stirner's rise from obscurity helps explain the controversy he stirs. His book *The Ego and Its Own*, published in 1844, was well reviewed, attracted considerable criticism and was banned by government censors in 1845 – yet for thirty-odd years it remained largely ignored. Stirner had laid the groundwork for his later notoriety as a member of the Young Hegelians, the philosophical circle that met in Berlin in the 1840s, where he became acquainted with Marx and Engels. Engels had regarded Stirner as a friend and Marx was sufficiently impressed in 1842 to publish two of Stirner's essays: *The False Principle of Our Education* and *Art and Religion*. Yet, working as a pair, Marx and Engels trashed Stirner's work. Perhaps also regarding him as a rival, they painted him as a hopelessly abstract, confused, bourgeois individualist, spitefully nicknaming him Saint Max.

What remains of their substantial critique of *The Ego and Its Own* takes up the best part of the *German Ideology*, a manuscript produced in 1845 but not published until 1932. A vulgarised version of their critique was popularised in the 1890s just at the point that Stirner's ideas were being revived by the anti-communist anarchists Benjamin Tucker and, most importantly, John Henry Mackay. In 1895, the Marxist founder of the Russian Social Democratic Movement Georgi Plekhanov rehashed Marx and Engles' appraisal, this time stressing Stirner's affinity – as translator of Adam Smith and J. B. Say – with classical liberal political economy. Indeed, forging a link between egoism and laissez faire liberalism, Plekhanov praised Stirner as the "most consequent of anarchists" in order to damn all anarchists as irrevocably individualist. To make matters worse, Stirner was embraced at around the same time by ultra-conservatives who gravitated towards Cosima Wagner, the composer's anti-Semitic second wife and purveyor of German cultural and racial superiority. The idea that Stirner had anticipated Nietzsche's Ubermensch was quickly established (though there is scant evidence to suggest that Nietzsche had read Stirner). The effect was twofold: as well as adding an aristocratic lustre to the interpretation of the egoist and superman, it enabled writers in the post-war period to paint anarchism as a totalitarian, illiberal ideology. Anti-anarchist historians fascinated by the esteem that Proudhon enjoyed with proto-fascists in early twentieth-century France could now play with another intellectual lineage to build a bridge from anarchism to fascism.

Learning to love Stirner is not an uncomplicated task. With constant repetition, the assertion that egoism underpins anarchism has stuck, at least partially. Stirner's derision of Proudhon's declaration "property is theft" as priestly moralising hardly helps would-be friends rebut claims of his petite bourgeois inclinations. It's not surprising, then, that swathes of anarchist communists have preferred to accept the Marxist critique and remove Stirner from anarchism's history than mount a counter-attack or defence. Stirner's most vocal anarchist advocates have barely eased his rehabilitation. In the work of his followers, Stirner variously emerges as a neo-Hobbesian, hyper-liberal or joyful hedonist. In the first he appears as a proponent of the view that humans are, or should be, self-directed because life is necessarily a struggle between individuals for domination. In the second, he is an advocate of autonomy and endless pluralism. In the third, he champions the prohibition of prohibitions.

EGOISM: THE ANARCHIST'S DILEMMA

Stirner's greatness comes from the dilemma he creates for anarchists broadly attracted by his commitment to 'ownness' – his refusal to suspend individual judgment and his positive endorsement that individuals discover themselves and recover their uniqueness. In *The Ego and Its Own*, ownness involves a rejection of political and moral obligations: individuals should do nothing other than follow their will. Thus Stirner exhorts individuals to become egoists – this is the only good he recognises. Each must understand that the promise of freedom through the realisation of rights in the liberal state is illusory; each must take possession of itself to avoid being trapped by instinctual desires or automatic compliance with social norms. In one of his more provocative moments, Stirner argued that the radical "moral man" who never doubted "that the copulation of brother and sister is incest, that monogamy is the truth of marriage, that filial piety is a sacred duty" and shuddered at the idea of "being allowed to touch his sister as wife," remained ensnared by inherited rules that were not of his own making. Stirner professed complete indifference to the moral standards enshrined in law or social practice. Accordingly he styled the egoist as one able to stand aloof from convention. "Entitled or unentitled – that does not concern me, if I am only *powerful*, I am of myself *empowered*, and need no other empowering or entitling." While Kropotkin included Stirner in the anarchist family, he parted company with him on this point. Kropotkin believed that people should reflect on their moral codes. He endorsed the nihilist demand to scrutinise all values and the nihilists' refusal to observe conventions. But he did not accept that it was possible for individuals to detach themselves from their social contexts as Stirner suggested, and he believed that anarchists who attempted to do so were misguided.

The upside of Stirner's defence of egoism is his exhilarating critique of the state and the idea of the common good. The downside is that to live as egoists, individuals must reject all obligations and commitments beyond the dedication to egoism. The dilemma Stirner poses is about how far the anarchist rejection of political and moral obligations can and should be pushed.

HIERARCHY AND DOMINATION

Unlike the writers who dominated the Young Hegelians, Stirner was critical of the radical political project to reform the state along humanist lines. He identified this with the construction of the state and the idea of the nation and he argued that it would result in the replication of hierarchy and domination.

Stirner's critique extended from his scepticism about the emancipatory potential of political philosophy. The hope of philosophy was that the 'cultured' would be able to devise perfect social orders. Before the eighteenth century, it was self-consciously designed as an exercise in the mastery of the mind over matter by the cultured on behalf of the 'uncultured,' this latter group being the "animal mass" that was incapable of thinking independently, and which fell into line with the perfect orders the cultured invented. With Hegel, all this appeared to be changed. Philosophy obtained a new objectivity, uniting ideas with reality and overcoming the gap between ideal theory and material reality. For Stirner the change was deceptive. What happened was that philosophers got caught up in their own cleverness, and this rendered them insensible to the domination that mind now attained as the driver of social change. It appeared to the cultured that their favourite concepts were in fact real. Consequently, while the prospect of attaining perfection remained as compelling as ever, the mastery of mind was now concealed. "Hierarchy is the domination of thoughts, dominion of mind!" Stirner suggested that it reached unparalleled heights in the nineteenth century.

Humanism was the stuff of the philosophers' dreams. The same visions of the egalitarian community and brotherly love motivated political actors, too. Robespierre and St. Just, the leaders of the French revolution, dedicated themselves to the destruction of monarchical absolutism and the tyranny of the Catholic Church. Yet unable to escape the domination of mind, they created a new holy order to replace it. This centred on the idea of man. Man was not a person but a "spook" or a concept of a person who exhibited particular virtues, adopted a fixed set of values, and unselfishly struggled for the attainment of the social conditions that would enable real human beings to thrive – thus bringing reality in line with the ideal. What was the result? Stirner's pithy answer was: The Terror. "Because the revolutionary priests... served Man, they cut off the heads of men."

Stirner called the institutional form that corresponded to this humanist ideal liberalism. It could take liberal, social and humane forms. In the first rights were equalised; the second abolished property ownership; and the third unified faith. In equating liberalism with 'the State,' Stirner emphasised its stultifying uniformity. Whereas the state had once described a discrete group within the broader social unit, it now encapsulated the whole. Statists rejected factions, separate interests and difference. In the name of equality, they promoted the general over the particular and the common good over the well-being of the minority or the individual. Citizens accepted the state's levelling, even though it was utterly demeaning. Stirner used 'equality of rights' as an example. This doctrine was passed off as a principle of fairness, but it actually indicated that "the State has no regard for my person, that to it I, like every other, am only a man, without having another significance that commands its deference." Whichever of the "innumerable multitude of rights" states conferred – the "right to lead a battalion," the "right to lecture at a university" – each award confirmed the state's total disregard for the special qualities that right-holders possessed, and reinforced compliance with the conditions attached to the occupation of roles.

Citizens were duty-bound to advance the state's interests as their own even at their physical and psychological cost. State law was in any case implemented by physical force, but because state violence was normalised and neutralised as righteous punishment, transgression was necessarily internalised by citizens as criminality. The arch chicanery of the state was to advertise its guardianship of the very freedom it negated. Self-styled as the protector of liberties, the state became indispensable to humanity's flourishing. The inevitable upshot was that the state was compelled to prioritise its own interests over the citizenry. Political liberty was said to mean "*my* liberty" but translated into "the liberty of a power that rules and subjugates me." "State, religion, conscience" thus "make me a slave, and their liberty is my slavery." The state sanctified itself, following the principle of "the end hallows the means," and in this it was essentially Jesuitical, "moral." Stirner explained: "If the welfare of the State is the end, war is a hallowed means; if justice is the State's end, homicide is a hallowed means, and is called by its sacred name 'execution'; the sacred State hallows everything that is serviceable to it." Two maxims summed up his anarchist view: "Liberty of the people is not my liberty;" "Every State is a *despotism*."

PROMISING

Once asked how he reconciled his advocacy of Marxism-Leninism with the individualism of the Black Panthers, Eldridge Cleaver replied that all ideological systems were repressive and that "any constraint on our freedoms is not acceptable." The sentiment resonates with Stirner's egoism but it begs a question about the tools Stirner provided to support resistance or liberation.

Stirner's politics was anti-revolutionary, and insurrectionary. Explaining the difference he defined revolution as the effort to bring new arrangements into being and insurrection as the struggle against arrangements. Insurrection "leads us no longer to let ourselves be arranged, but to arrange ourselves." Christ was an insurrectionist. Preaching obedience and refusing to lead the Jews in revolt against their Roman masters, he created mayhem simply by attending to himself rather than to others and treading his own path "untroubled about and undisturbed" by the authorities. Christ was an "insurgent," the "deadly enemy" and "real annihilator." Refusing to acknowledge the state's claims, he constructed his own rules independently of it and so revealed its emptiness.

Stirner suggested that egoism was compatible with combined action and talked of "all slaves" attaining their freedom. He also imagined the "union of egos." This coalition would take shape from the "incessant self-uniting" activity of egos, encouraging fluid, impermanent relationships within the body of dead society; however, while the egoist could take part in gatherings, social bonds were disallowed – egoism meant disregarding the interests of others. Here Stirner's ideal diverged markedly from any traditional view of Christ's mission: "What you have the *power* to be you have the *right* to. I derive all right and all warrant from me; I am entitled to everything that I have in my power."

There was no love, for this entailed sacrifice and demanded 'self-sacrifice' in turn. Nor was community possible. This was a fiction or spook and Stirner insisted that it required egos to enter into relationships that were enslaving. Egoists should forego it, appropriate the state's powers and exercise them exclusively for their own satisfaction. Others were "only means and organs which we may use as our property!" The fatally injured woman who strangled her child in order to die 'satisfied' was an exemplar. She did not let love – either for her child or the community it may have enriched – get the better of her will. Promising was likewise impossible. Were "I to be bound to-day and henceforth to my will of yesterday" my "will would... be *frozen*." Promising made the ego "a bondman," a "willer yesterday" and "to-day without a will: yesterday voluntary, to-day involuntary." The road to freedom lay in "recognizing no *duty*, not *binding* myself nor letting myself be bound."

MAX STIRNER

PIERRE-JOSEPH PROUDHON

Proudhon is famous for two reasons. First, he's the author of *What is Property?* the book containing the immortal phrase "property is theft!" Second, he has emerged as the 'first' anarchist. This accolade is explained in part by his provocative reclamation of 'anarchy.' Until Proudhon published his critique of property in 1840 the term had only been applied pejoratively. In the other part, it comes from his encounter with Marx. In 1846 Proudhon rebuffed Marx's tentative advances and hinted that he found his proposals dogmatic. Proudhon died in 1865 and was not party to the disputes that led to the subdivision of the international socialist movement; nevertheless, his early promotion of anarchy established him as the originator of the anti-authoritarian current that opposed Marxist socialism in the 1860s and 70s.

Proudhon's greatness is sometimes linked to his political economy and his advocacy of decentralised federation, namely: organising 'from the bottom up' and on the basis of free agreement or voluntary association. His federalist ideas were profoundly influential in nineteenth-century left-liberal and anti-authoritarian circles, notably in Spain, where anti-monarchist revolutionaries actively promoted Proudhonian principles from the late 1860s. During the same period, Proudhon was one of the best known social philosophers of the age, often compared to Kant and Hegel. His early admirers included Mikhail Bakunin, who honoured Proudhon as the "master of us all," and Alexander Herzen, Bakunin's compatriot and sometime friend.

Editing a series of four papers in France during and after the 1848 revolution, Proudhon exercised an enormous influence on French workers, lending his name to a mass movement. Marx later heaped ridicule on Proudhon's economics and seemingly shaky grasp of Hegelian dialectics. His star plummeted as Marx's rose and its re-ascendance was for many years frustrated by the paucity of English-language translations of his work. Proudhon's designation as an 'individualist' rather than 'communist' anarchist, notably by his late-nineteenth and early twentieth-century champion Benjamin Tucker, probably also slowed his rehabilitation. Most of all, Proudhon's reputation has been badly tarnished by his anti-Semitism and anti-feminism. Anarchists on both sides of the individualist-communist divide have expressed alarm at the depth of Proudhon's cultural prejudice and his adoption by some twentieth-century ultra-right and fascist groups. His professed anti-feminism is frequently described as misogynist. Proudhon regarded women's rights as an 'absolute' demand, incompatible with his social philosophy. As Louise Michel noted, the practical upshot of this vaunted position was that he classified women either as domestics or whores.

Proudhon is not the only anarchist with a blemished record. He remains a great anarchist not just because he bequeathed later activists a socio-political framework for the organisation of anarchy but above all because he outlined an approach to philosophy, science and sociology that pinned law and certainty to the idea that everything in social life is fluid and contingent. Proudhon gave anarchists de-centralised federalism as an approach to pluralism and power, not as an organisational principle.

THE PHILOSOPHY OF PROGRESS

Born in Besançon in 1809, Proudhon shared his birthplace with the utopian socialist Charles Fourier and the republican writer Victor Hugo. Yet he did not place himself in a Bisontin radical tradition or assume the mantle of either of the town's famous sons. Proudhon's thinking about the centrality of labour to social transformation picked up on a prominent theme in Fourier's utopian socialism, but he mocked Fourier's work when he first came across it while training as a proof-corrector and compositor in the late 1820s. Proudhon was more attuned to Hugo. His hostility to Napoleon III, which led to his arrest in 1849, was as fierce as Hugo's and similarly rooted in a critique of arbitrary rule. Nevertheless, while Proudhon regarded Hugo as a political ally, he considered that his own original contribution to human understanding lay in philosophy not politics, specifically in his exposition of the philosophy of progress.

Movement was Proudhon's core concept and it operated in two ways. First, Proudhon argued that everything in nature and social life existed in a state of constant change. Planets, orders, people, practices, norms, thought (what he called Reason) were all subject to movement. Second, movement established relations between things. It assumed that there were points of departure or principles and points of arrival or aims. Describing movement as a law of existence, Proudhon argued that nothing that the law described, including reason, possessed fixed content. 'Nature,' 'the individual,' 'society' were all perceptions, products of the imagination or what he called 'fictions.' It was possible to describe and analyse them but it was impossible to break them down into their component parts, either to discover their essence or deduce their ideal operating conditions. Nor was it possible to discover their ultimate cause. Cause or force was merely a property of movement that animated principles to realise aims.

Proudhon set progress against the Absolute and absolutism, referring to any notion of intransigence. At a high level this included theological conceptions of God and the derivative idea of obedience to a single sovereign. Movement spelt "the negation of every immutable form and formula, of every doctrine of eternity, permanence, impeccability," and progress was "the negation of every permanent order, even that of the universe, and of every subject or object, empirical or transcendental, which does not change." Proudhon's law unsettled the foundations of traditional philosophy while recognising its ideational force and transformative potential. On one side of the equation, movement undermined notions of eternal power, original creation and superior will, and denied the existence of a perfect deity against which humans were reckoned sullied and imperfect. On the other, it affirmed God's creation through religious observance and declared God's becoming as a force for humanity's cultivation. Proudhon thus cleared the way for Bakunin's demand for God's abolition and Tolstoy's recognition of the kingdom of God within.

Anticipating Foucault, Proudhon once remarked that he never re-read his work and had forgotten most of what he had written. Unruffled by the prospect of critique, he wore his probable errors and inconsistencies as a badge of honour. Better to inspire others than push would-be followers to venerate texts or pour over them to divine doctrine. System and systematising were to be deplored. Only absolutists insisted on perfection and staunch consistency. Moreover, the pursuit of the ideal was dangerous. It resulted in the confusion of conception with principle and development with existence, encouraging the prescription of models as permanent cures for everyone's ills. Proudhon detected absolutism in the centralisation of the Ancien Régime and equally in Jean-Jacques Rousseau's reflections on the human condition, human corruption and moral polity. He also saw it in the bourgeoisie's consolidation of power in 1789 and the class advantages it subsequently anchored in the constitution.

Vulgar philosophers typically associated progress with cumulative improvement, another kind of absolutism, variously assessed using measures of certainty, civility, equality, market expansion, technological advance and increased happiness. Proudhon embraced some of these phenomena but rejected the formulation of historical advance and the sciences it spawned. If absolutists applied philosophy as snake oil, the philosophy of progress was not a new brew. It was a critique that focussed attention on the articulation of a positive science of the material world.

EXCHANGE AND ECONOMY

Proudhon turned to sociology and political economy to investigate the nefarious effects of absolutism. His leading assumptions were, first, that society emerged from human interaction and, second, that labour was the basis of interaction. Society was an order of free exchange spontaneously constituted by the "fluid relations and economic solidarity of all of the individuals, of the nation, of the locality or corporation, or of the entire species." In society "individuals circulate freely," make approaches, "join together" and disperse "in turn, in all directions." Anarchy was the order of society and was natural and perfectible in this sense alone:

"Society exists from the day that individuals, communicating by labor and speech, assume reciprocal obligations and give birth to laws and customs. Undoubtedly society becomes perfect in proportion to the advances of science and economy, but at no epoch of civilisation does progress imply any such metamorphosis as those dreamed of by the builders of utopia; and however excellent the future condition of humanity is to be, it will be none the less the natural continuation, the necessary consequence, of its previous positions."

When society was made subject to absolutist principles, social relationships were invariably distorted and constrained. Proudhon focused on the regulatory systems introduced by social elites, namely capitalists and landowners, where property ownership was guaranteed as an exclusive right, to highlight the effects on the economy: production was geared towards profit, work was performed to exhaustion, technology was used destructively, land enjoyed as a marker of status, and taxation imposed as a cosh to maintain the panoply of policing the system required.

Proudhon's recommendations for reform were extensive. The list included the abolition of rent and interest; the abandonment of credit; the introduction of reciprocal exchange; the liquidation of debts and mortgages; and tax and tariff reform. This package of practical proposals described the theory of mutualism and Proudhon argued that its realisation would reduce the role of centralised government, rebalancing the power of society against the state. Mutualism dispensed with the plethora of coercive measures adopted to ensure the state's smooth functioning. It also facilitated democratisation, which Proudhon associated with anarchy, demanding social restructuring.

This contestation of absolutism was progressive because it recovered transitory concepts from the static principles of political economy and pioneered a form of organisation robust enough to maintain the balance of forces active in society without over-prescribing rules of interaction. Proudhon's approach reversed the logic of recuperation: his conception approximated more closely to the idea of recovery from illness than to commodification or loss. Noting that principles of competition and monopoly were used by political economists to rationalise exclusivity, individual advantage and social disintegration, Proudhon maintained that these concepts were equally tools to advance liberty. Monopoly was only "the autocracy of man over himself," the "dictatorial right accorded by nature to every producer of using his faculties as he pleases, of giving free play to his thought in whatever direction it prefers." Competition, likewise, was "the expression of collective activity" productive of social solidarity.

Distinguishing himself from absolutist reformers, notably Jacobins and old-time communists who dreamed of using the machinery of the state to bring exchange under the direct control of self-appointed, benevolent elites, Proudhon denied that de-centralisation and federation amounted to a system of government. Having witnessed Napoleon III's Caesarist manoeuvring and the success of the 1851 coup, he was alert to the vulnerability of the anarchist orders he championed. Unlike the state, society was necessarily plural and diverse. It achieved social harmony by allowing competing forces to act upon each other, not by inculcating unitary ideals. It was possible, then, to imagine an authoritarian charge against anarchy and the re-regulation of society by conservatives, zealots of laissez-faire liberalism or communists. Federalism was Proudhon's solution. It reinforced the equalities and solidarities that mutualism underwrote. Parties to the federation entered into contracts to guarantee mutual care and well-being. This preserved individual sovereignty and rights while creating reciprocal obligations to ensure that progress – "the railway of liberty" – was protected from resurgent absolutist fantasies.

MOTORS OF CHANGE

Convention has it that war is productive of order. War made the state and the state made war and justice developed from the conflicts. Proudhon's modification of this relation preserved what he called the right of force, but tacked it to the law of movement and dispensed with the criteria of judgement victors habitually used to moralise the orders they established.

Resurrecting the old warrior spirit to defend the right of force, Proudhon recognised its debasement by the structural power advantages that states protected. There was no honour in the institutionalised civil wars owners waged against workers or in the militarised international adventures they financed to further their economic interests; however, seeing force as an essential component of the law of movement, he believed that it animated competition and the interactions that stimulated unity without atrophy. In society, individuals exercised unequal force against each other and within the collectives they were members of in order to assert their individuality. Although their association was natural and spontaneous, human beings were not bees or ants. They did not occupy predetermined or stable roles within their associations. Indeed, human organisation assumed unsettled division and the differentiation of the individual from the whole. Individuals were socialised in society but also exercised an independent force on it. There was an irreducible tension between the two. Force was the glue that held social relations in equilibrium. Social health was measured by the gentleness of the oscillations required to achieve equilibrium and social disease by the potency of the force required to maintain balance.

Reviewing ancient society from his nineteenth-century vantage-point, Proudhon suggested that the moderns were more honest, livelier and equipped with a greater respect for rights. Yet he refused to link justice to moral precept or standard. The concept of justice and the idea of moral law were supreme. But these too emerged from force and social struggle. Justice was the struggle for the sublime, the cultivation of perfection through art, politics, philosophy, music and physical prowess. Previous generations had wrongly created external standards of perfection, elaborated against humanity. Proudhon believed that perfection demanded the jettisoning of these idols and ideals. The deification of man progressed by imagination and invention: "nothing remains for us to take; the tradition is exhausted: we are forced to become original in our turn, and to continue the movement."

LUCY PARSONS

———

I n 1900, a Republican-leaning US local broadsheet crowned Lucy Parsons an anarchist queen. The coronation bucked a trend. The press usually referred to her as the widow of Albert Parsons, one of the anarchists executed in 1887 following the bombing of a labour demonstration in Chicago's Haymarket Square. The coupling was not entirely inappropriate. Having spearheaded the defence campaigns for the accused, she frequently referred to the injustice of the trial to spotlight the steeliness of capitalist 'slavocracy'; however, her association with Albert is easily misconstrued: she never played second fiddle to Albert nor stood in his shadow. She was a talented writer, orator and organiser in her own right.

A keen advocate of independent labour organising in the late nineteenth century, Parsons was active in the Knights of Labor and the anarchist International Working People's Association. In 1905, she joined the Industrial Workers of the World (IWW). She wrote regularly for the anarchist-socialist press and lectured across America, refusing to be cowed by police bans or arrests for riot that followed as a consequence of her defiance. In 1888, she spoke at a Haymarket memorial rally in London, leaving a deep impression on the anarchists in William Morris' Socialist League. As 'head' of the Chicago Reds, Parsons was to Chicago what Louise Michel was to Paris, and her influence, like Michel's, extended well beyond the city's limits.

Like most anarchists of the period, Parsons was forever asked questions about political violence and terrorist tactics. Deeply concerned about the capacity of the print media to shape public perceptions, she scrupulously avoided reductive analysis. In a widely syndicated interview published after President McKinley's assassination in 1901, she ventured that the assailant, Leon Czolgosz, was mentally ill. If this sounded like straightforward censure, Parsons based her diagnosis on his evident misunderstanding of class power. She judged Czolgosz deluded because he had wrongly thought there was something to be gained from the shooting. Anyone in their right mind could see that he had mistaken the symbol for the source. It was the trusts and heads of trusts who wielded real power, not the people's temporary chief executives.

Parsons' qualified critique reflected her general view that 'organised' government was in the pay of economic lobbyists and therefore largely insulated from its electors. Her refusal to condemn political violence, even as anti-anarchist hysteria reached fever-pitch, also reflected an eagerness to resist binary tactics. Parsons once argued that there were two main categories of anarchist: militant and philosophical. The latter were agitators and teachers who believed in organisation. Militants eschewed organisation and believed in independent action, each one choosing their own path. Gaetano Bresci, assassin of King Umberto I, was an example of this type. Parsons described herself as an 'old school' anarchist because she advocated formal organisation to support sustained propaganda. Organisation was essential for the construction of movements capable of withstanding capitalist intimidation, infiltration and vigilante actions: without it workers were easy prey for the bosses. Yet Parsons had a foot in both camps and appreciated the galvanising power of the individual act. Her 1884 clarion call, *Word to Tramps*, declared that "organization would be a detriment" to those willing to petition the rich with explosives. Similarly, in 1900 she participated in the Bresci solidarity meeting, backing the appeal for workingmen to "come in crowds." For Parsons the chief enemy was inertia. As she put it: "Passivity while slavery is stealing over us is a crime."

CLASS WAR

Born to an enslaved woman in 1851, Parsons explored class conflict through the prism of the American Civil War. When she spoke about the war she referred to the brutality of the fighting, the nobility of the cause and the bitterness of its betrayal. It had been waged to end oppression, for liberation and to put an end to enslavement. For Parsons, this meant abolishing both chattel slavery and the structural oppressions it epitomised. Only one of these aims had been realised: Abraham Lincoln had emancipated the slaves but the oppression continued. Returning home from the battlefields the ordinary soldiers discovered that "bloated aristocracy" and "crude monied-ocracy" had won the day and that their lives now hinged on the benevolence of the "slimy cowards" who had made a fast buck from turning out their "paste-bottom boots" – "The overseer's whip is now fully supplanted by the lash of hunger! And the auction block by the chain gang and the convict cell!"

When Ulysses Grant accepted Robert E. Lee's surrender to bring the hostilities to a formal end, the war rumbled on. Parsons observed that the political settlement signalled an important realignment of forces and a change in tactics. Having settled the issue of individual property rights, slavers on both sides of the Confederate-Unionist divide regrouped, forging new alliances to wage covert war against the veterans who had done their killing and anyone else who attempted to resist enslavement. Dispensing with the heavy artillery, the owners now wielded the state's constitutional powers, elaborate electoral machinery, the "lying monopolistic press," Pinkerton private militias and armed police to quell resistance. This was class war. It appeared less gruesome than the pitched battles that characterised the Civil War but the oppressors pursued it with the same viciousness. Parsons addressed black workers to explain:

"The same land which you once tilled as a chattel slave you still till as a wage-slave, and in the same cabin which you then entered at eve not knowing but what you would be sold from wife and little ones before the morrow's setting sun, you now enter with dread lest you will be slain by the assassin hand of those who once would have sold you if they did not like you."

In fact, whereas the Civil War had been fought with honour, the class war was waged shamefully. Unlike General Grant, who accepted Lee's capitulation magnanimously, the state of Illinois ran Albert Parsons through when he gave himself up for trial. It was reasonable to assume that the amnesties that the Union granted the rebels in the Reconstruction era would never be extended to the anarchists and their allies who resisted the new arrangements. Workers should draw their own conclusions. Referring to the 1886 killing spree in Carrolton, Mississippi, which resulted in 23 deaths, Parsons told her black audience:

"As to those local, periodical, damnable massacres to which you are at all times liable, these you must revenge in your own way. Are you deaf, dumb and blind to the atrocities that you are subjected to? Have the gaping wounds of your dead comrades become so common that they no longer move you? Is your heart a heart of stone, or its palpitations of those of cowards, that you slink to your wretched abode and offer no resistance... Do you need more

horrible realities than these to goad you on to deeds
of revenge that will at least make your oppressors
dread you?"

Parsons described the class war as a war against Christian
civilisation. It had three fronts. One was against the system
of economic and industrial robbery that enabled capitalists
to claim ownership of the things that workers produced,
from everyday consumables to the astonishing buildings that
fashioned the city skylines. The second was the 'organised
fraud' of government. Happy people, she argued, needed no
government and were instead inclined towards individualism,
or "real self-government." Take away the complex systems
required to maintain the injustice of capitalist oppression
and people would order themselves. The third front was
against religion. Parsons understood this in a narrow sense
to refer to the hypocrisy of Church leaders who taught one
set of ethics and practiced another, and in a broad sense
to refer to the ideology of equal opportunity and the myth
of classlessness that pervaded America. Parsons knew from
walking the streets of New York and Chicago that workers
lived in abject poverty, packed "like sardines" into squalid
tenements on filthy sidewalks, and that their children had
no access to the parks and amenities that adorned the areas
uptown. The picture was one of despair "at once degrading,
disgusting and depressing." Making do with "coffee wagons
and soup kitchens" and taking the charity that the "robber
class" handed out "like dope" to keep them quiet, they
desperately poured over the job adverts that peppered the

yellow press, also absorbing the messages that instructed them to cling tightly to the American dream.

CLASS AND SOLIDARITY

Parsons believed that all workers were exploited by capitalists but she also argued that the experience of exploitation was felt more or less sharply by sub-sets of workers. In other words, gender and race operated independently of class as determinants of oppression.

Women had long been regarded as inferior to men, turned into household drudges and tolerated on condition that they provided their masters with progeny. Some twentieth-century "new women" were able to venture outside the domestic sphere, receive education and enjoy independence. They did not lack inspiring role models to help them make their way: Louise Michel was one. She shone "like a pillar of light or a star of hope." Still, most women remained "man-tagged." The better-educated were often groomed for domestic service and waitressing, where social norms dictated that applicants should be under forty, good-looking and "wholesome." For the rest, life remained a grind. In her visits to the city ghettos, Parsons noted the relationship between hardship and childrearing: the more "poverty-stricken the appearance of the women the greater number of children they seem to have clinging to their skirts."

Women were exploited "more ruthlessly than the men" simply because they were women. They were the "slaves of the slaves." Similarly, black Americans were regarded as inferior to whites and routinely subject to racist abuse and violence. At the time of the Carrolton massacre, Parsons maintained that the violence had not been racially motivated: relative poverty was the more important explanatory factor. Black workers in the South were "poorer as a class" than their "white wage-slave" brothers in the North. By 1892 she had changed her mind. Hearing news of the lynchings then reaching a peak in the South, she compared American racist violence to Russian anti-Semitism. As vulnerable as the Jews were under Tsarism, their sufferings were as nothing compared to "lashings and lynching" taking place across the old rebel states. Parsons reported that "leering, white-skinned, black-hearted brutes" stripped women bare, beat them insensible and "strangled them from the limbs of trees." This was race war, intensified by gender discrimination and class hatred.

Parsons' analysis of oppression was reflected in her understanding of solidarity. It had four aspects. First, solidarity was process. Workers had to learn how to exert collective force, build "solidarity of interest as a mass" and act as a class. Second, the process involved distinguishing between class interest and class membership. While it was impossible to reconcile workers' and owners' interests, it was nevertheless possible for individuals to transcend economic class divisions. Florence Nightingale, one of

Parson's "famous women of history," blazed this trail. "Far from want" she had risked her wellbeing to "bring relief to that most stupid victim or our present system, the soldier." In doing so, she had demonstrated solidarity of interest with the oppressed. Third, solidarity meant standing firm with workers who apparently betrayed class interest, notably scabs. These workers were not to be despised: a scab was just a "poverty-stricken, disheartened wage-slave." Solidarity demanded that workers refuse to handle scabbed goods but also that they heal the divisions that owners' created within the mass movement. Fourth, solidarity meant supporting independent organisation and leadership within the workers' movements. Endorsing the words of an anonymous black anti-racist organiser, Parsons noted: "The white race furnished us one John Brown; the next must come from our own race."

WAR AND PEACE

Parsons believed that there could be no peace without liberation and that workers were always right to resist exploitation and oppression. She never revised her conception of class war and she scoffed at those who preached peace as a strategic response to domination. Why was "lamb-like" behaviour demanded only of workers and never owners: "Why should they be quiet while starving or receiving just sufficient for their laborious toil to keep body and soul together and to produce more slaves for the bosses?" Yet towards the end of her life she concluded that she was unlikely to witness the demise of capitalism as she had once anticipated. Her frank assessment was that anarchism remained "too far away from the mental level of the masses." Anti-anarchist propaganda was partly to blame. It was easy for the authorities to paint anarchism as dangerous and unruly; Parsons' own rhetoric was perhaps misjudged in this respect. But rather than change tack or blame the opposition, she invited anarchists to acknowledge their own deficiencies: they had failed to sustain organisations essential for the promotion of anarchist ideas.

Parsons' late speeches often harked back to Haymarket. There was some nostalgia in this but a larger dose of hope. Haymarket was a historical trigger for the righteous anger and indignation government smothered. At a wildcat May Day rally in 1930, as the US economy hurtled toward collapse, she warmed to the sight of "young people... who will drop work... when work is so scarce... come out in the mid-week and defy the capitalist classes... come out in the sunlight... standing solid for shorter hours and better conditions... those are the kind of people we have got to have."

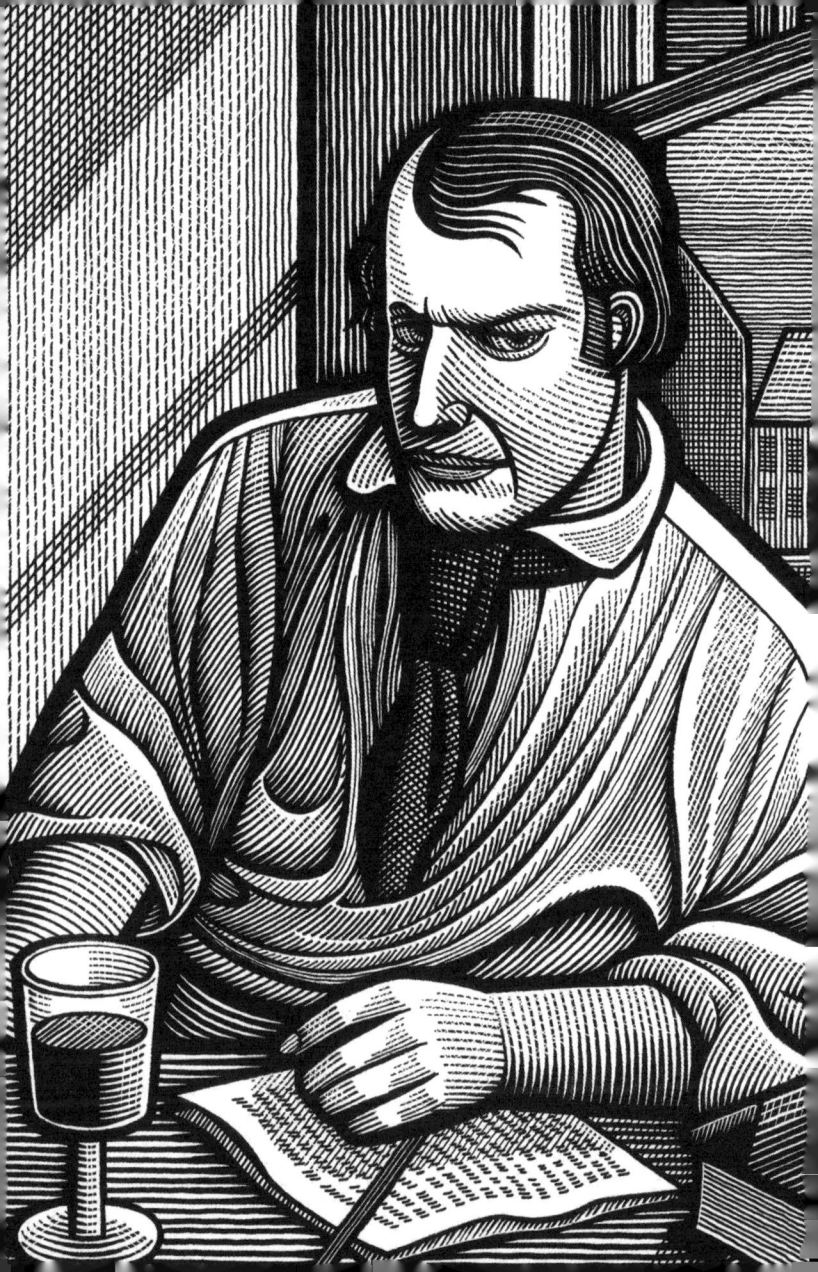

WILLIAM GODWIN

G odwin was an eighteenth-century radical writer and journalist and one of the leading participants in the debates sparked by the French Revolution. An ally of Tom Paine, he was also a critic of Edmund Burke, the Whig-cum-conservative author of *Reflections on the Revolution in France*. Godwin shared Burke's abhorrence of The Terror but wholly rejected his glowing defence of aristocracy. At first enthusiastic about the Revolution, Godwin made two lasting interventions into revolutionary debates: the theoretical treatise *Political Justice* and the novel *Caleb Williams*.

Godwin is sometimes credited with being the first philosophical anarchist, a claim that has perhaps created a misleading impression that he was an engaging armchair-critic or that his contribution to radical politics rests on the rigour of his system, best assessed by its strict, logical dissection. These approaches simultaneously underplay the active role he took in politics and the character of the philosophy he advanced. Like many of his contemporaries, Godwin understood publishing as a form of activism, an intervention into public debate that was intended to shape it and which also entailed risk. Godwin suggested that *Political Justice* escaped censorship because it was judged too expensive to inflame public debate, but it sold in the thousands and was read widely in the political societies that mushroomed across the country in the 1790s. As activists turned to the book to press for democratic change, Godwin went out of his way to protest the arrest of friends and fellow radicals on charges of treason, and to defend rights of free speech, the press, and assembly, curtailed by the government's Gagging Acts. Similarly, when it came to political philosophy, Godwin was as disparaging of ideal systems as Proudhon. Perfectibility meant the capacity to improve, not the achievement of perfection. This ruled against the discovery of model political orders – such as Rousseau's *Social Contract*, the text that animated the French Jacobins – as well as habitual reliance on precepts derived from logic or faith. As he explained: "to rest in general rules is sometimes a necessity which our imperfection imposes upon us" but "the true dignity of human reason is, as much as we are able, to go beyond them, to have our faculties … act upon every occasion that occurs, and to correct ourselves accordingly." Judgment and experience were the proper guides to action, not reason or law.

Today, Godwin is as likely to be remembered for his family connections as he is for his independent contributions to radical politics. He married Mary Wollstonecraft in 1797, five years after she published her best-known book,

A Vindication of the Rights of Woman. She died the same year, after giving birth to their daughter Mary, the future author of Frankenstein. His influence was felt strongly in and through the writing of his son-in-law, the Romantic revolutionary poet, Percy Bysshe Shelley. Yet with the exception of Kropotkin, who identified him as the first person to set out an anarchist doctrine, he was barely read by later anarchists. In recent times, Tom Paine has emerged as the eighteenth-century champion of anarchistic thought, though he probably aligns more easily with left republicanism. It was Godwin who distinguished himself as the critic of government. This "boasted institution," he said, "is nothing more than a scheme for enforcing by brute violence the sense of one man or set of men upon another." He did not call his critique anarchist, but as Kropotkin later argued, aspects of Godwin's thought resonated with the overt anarchism that Proudhon and others advanced after 1840.

ANARCHY AND SELF-GOVERNMENT

Godwin presented two views of anarchy, one negative and one hopeful. The negative conception came from the common understanding of anarchy as the absence of government. In this guise it was as a condition of disorder, usually less attractive than established social orders. This view was reminiscent of the state of nature depicted by Thomas

Hobbes; however, Godwin departed from Hobbes in two ways. First, Godwin explained the nasty, brutish insecurity of anarchy as a result of unrestrained passion, not a lack of universal moral standards. Second, Godwin's anarchists are not atomised egos programmed to compete for power until they die, as Hobbes's are. They are excited by a sudden lack of restraint and so "grasp at power" in a "rigorous, unfeeling and fierce" manner. Against Hobbes, Godwin concluded that it was impossible to imagine an idea "more pregnant with absurdity" than that "of a whole people taking arms against each other till they are all exterminated."

In Godwin's view, anarchy is an uncivil condition, not an asocial one. It was a "short lived mischief" – akin to a revolutionary uprising – that led to the temporary suspension of reason, and so undermined virtue. Yet his greatest fear of anarchy was that it cleared a path to despotism and tyranny by enabling despots to package the "horrible calamity" of anarchy as an incurable failure of self-government. "Men rendered mad with oppression, and drunk with the acquisition of new born power" were judged incapable of exercising "rational functions." In fact despotism usually explained these momentary suspensions of virtue and reason. Pressing home the point about the Hobbesian construction, Godwin noted: "it is to despotism that anarchy is indebted for its sting. If despotism were not ever watchful for its prey, and mercilessly prepared to take advantage of the errors of mankind, this ferment ... being left to itself, would subside into an even, clear and delightful calm."

Rejecting the despotic construction, Godwin argued that anarchy had a positive face. It may result, he argued, in "the best form of human society." In this sense, it could be likened to "true liberty" and defined as a vehicle for justice and virtue; it was usually generated by "the hatred of oppression" and "a spirit of independence" that "disengages men from prejudice and implicit faith."

Ordinary observations of human behaviours indicated that this positive form of anarchy was entirely practical. Rejecting the idea that law made people good, Godwin argued it was always coercive. Similarly, he believed that the threats posed by law-breakers were minimal, though they were often exaggerated. Every community sheltered a few children "of riot and plunder" but it was only the "satirical and censorious" who believed that their conduct cast a "general slur and aspersion" on the "whole species."

> "When we look at human society with kind and complacent survey, we are more than half tempted to imagine that men might subsist very well in clusters and congregated bodies without the coercion of law; and in truth criminal laws were only made to prevent the ill-disposed few from interrupting the regular and inoffensive proceedings of the vast majority."

Godwin's theoretical outlook may appear old-fashioned. The problems that occupied him turned on the promotion of virtue and enhancement of reason in a violent, corrupted and prejudiced world; however, his argument speaks to problems of structurelessness arising from the exercise of power without constraint and to the collapse or destruction of existing social orders, creating political vacuums for tyranny to fill. Godwin explored the virtues of anarchy as a practical reformer, not an ideologue. His view was that anarchy required the control of dominating behaviours to check potential mischief. Instead of presenting a choice between rule and no-rule, he outlined the tension arising from government and self-government. His conclusion was that refusing self-government was unjust and that self-government "imperfect as it is" was "more salutary than any thing that can be substituted in its place."

OBEDIENCE AND SELF-GOVERNMENT

In the notes for the projected second part of his semi-autobiographical novel *The First Man*, Albert Camus wrote: "Learning justice and morality means to decide whether an emotion is good or bad according to consequences." Godwin argued similarly and *Political Justice* gives considerable space to the discussion of improvement, education and pedagogy as a result. He also shared Camus' commitment to "autonomy" and his demand for "independence in interdependence." Yet Godwin talked about obedience in preference to using Camus' term and his concept of independence was strict. His "simple truth" was that "no man can in no case be bound to yield obedience to any other man or set of men upon earth."

Rather than measure freedom against obedience, Godwin distinguished between three types: voluntary, forced and habitual. Turning to the first, he described voluntary actions as acts of obedience because they conformed to our judgments, conscience or reason, formed in a social context. The obedience driven by our independent judgment was qualitatively different from the second type: repressive obedience. Godwin associated this with inequality, the desire to secure someone's approval or, even more starkly, avoid punishment. These were all destructive forms and they were linked to uneven distributions of property, wealth differentials and the cultural biases and social hierarchies that went hand-in-hand with economic injustice. Godwin depicted the relationship in *Caleb Williams*. When the anti-hero Williams discovers that his master, Falkland, is a murderer and requests that he be allowed to leave his service, the furious, diminished Falkland tells him that he will forever remain a slave to his whims:

> "You shall never quit it with your life. If you attempt it, you shall never cease to rue your folly as long as you exist. That is my will; and I will not have it resisted. The very next time you disobey me in that or any other article, there is an end of your vagaries for ever …
>
> Do not imagine I am afraid of you! I wear an armour, against which all your weapons are impotent. I have dug a pit for you; and whichever way you move … it is

ready to swallow you ... If once you fall, call as loud as you will, no man on earth shall hear your cries: Your innocence shall be of no service ... I laugh at so feeble a defence. It is as I say it; you may believe what I tell you."

Godwin distinguished the third type of obedience from these two. This came from what he called "confidence" and it was similar to the authority of the expert that Bakunin later discussed and allowed. Godwin disagreed, using the example of the builder and the mechanic to discuss the interdependent relation that Bakunin identified in the skill of the shoemaker and the dependency he feared in the specialist knowledge of the scientist. The problem with this kind of obedience, Godwin argued, was that the obedient not only sought the help of the expert but also learned to defer to their judgments and submit to their directions. Whether the skill was practical or intellectual, the harm was the same.

For Godwin, any departure "from the independence of our understanding," which "general and unlimited confidence necessarily includes," was to be resisted. The obedience instilled through confidence was always generally pernicious. It was one thing to be forced to obey a master for fear of the consequences but quite another to give up private judgement and common deliberation. In contrast to habitual obedience, repressive obedience did not entail the loss of independence. As Williams tells Falkland when his master eventually manages to send him to prison: "I am henceforth to be deprived of the benefits of integrity and honour. I am to forfeit the friendship of every one I have hitherto known, and to be precluded from the power of acquiring that of others." Yet facing a life of dishonour and disgrace, Williams adds, "If I am to despair of the good will of other men, I will at least maintain the independence of my own mind."

RESPECT AND TOLERATION

If Godwin anticipated do-it-yourself ethics, he remained suspicious of do-it-ourselves. The kind of independence he valued was rooted in freedom of expression and thought. This assumed community but also a delicate relationship between individuals and the whole. Godwin believed that individuals had a duty to advance the common good but rejected the imposition of contracts, promises and oaths to ensure compliance with abstract ideals. Marriage was an example. Although Godwin married Mary Wollstonecraft, apparently to save her from social censure for mothering an illegitimate child, he described it as the worst of all laws. Represented as a protection against "brutal lust and depravity," in reality, marriage assumed that women were rightfully men's property and that men were entitled to be "loved and esteemed" irrespective of their behaviours. More generally, promises and oaths merely concealed the violence necessary to coerce people to adopt unattractive conventions. "If the laws depend on promises for their execution," Godwin asked, "why are they accompanied by sanctions?"

Godwin believed in social progress and "the advancement of mind." "That which is today a considerable melioration, will at some future period, if preserved unaltered, appear a defect and disease in the body politic." Government lacked the "elasticity" to encourage progress and human beings, always imperfect, were also prone to regressive behaviours. Religion, democracy and party politics were some of the forces that encouraged individuals to band together to force others to do their bidding. Virtue sprang from intellect not conformity so it followed that self-government expressed common purpose, not collective action, and that it demanded mutual respect and toleration:

> "Toleration, and freedom of opinion, are scarcely worth accepting, if, when my neighbour differs from me, I do not indeed burn him, but I take every occasion to insult him. There could be no freedom of opinion, if every one conducted himself thus. Toleration ... requires, not only that there shall be no laws to restrain opinion, but that forbearance and liberality shall be moulded into the manners of the community."

WILLIAM GODWIN

ERRICO MALATESTA

Malatesta is the direct link between the demise of the First International in 1871 and the struggle against European fascism that started some forty years later. After the ruckus between Marx and Bakunin catalysed the separate development of revolutionary socialist organisations, he joined both the anarchist Federalist International and its Italian section. Spending long stretches of time in exile, dodging arrest and escaping jail, he lived much of his life like the great white shark, permanently on the move. Though there were periods of settlement in Italy, Argentina and the UK, he travelled widely in Europe, equally in its northern regions and along its Mediterranean shore, and made trips to Egypt, the US and Cuba. Wherever he happened to be, he always played a prominent role in Italian anarchist politics, editing a series of highly influential newspapers. He also wrote one of the movement's best loved pamphlets. Malatesta was present at the key international gatherings of the period, including the 1896 London meeting of the Second International, where he reportedly delivered a 'fiery speech' protesting the decision to eject anarchists from its congresses. In debates between organisationalists and individualists he sided with the former. Yet he stood in solidarity with his opponents to help frustrate police actions. A communist, he was pragmatic rather than doctrinaire and though he also advocated workers' self-organisation, he was cautious about syndicalism.

Malatesta was catapulted into public view in the UK in 1912, in the aftermath of the siege of Sidney Street. This was a stand-off in London's East End between a team of expropriators, several hundred police, and 120 troops, which sparked a moral panic about immigrants and calls for the habitual arming of the police. The troops had been deployed by Churchill, then Home Secretary, who was looking for fun and eager to demonstrate the government's resolve to kill criminal foreigners in front of a battalion of photo-journalists and Pathé news cameras. Malatesta's sale of a bottle of gas to one of the gang was enough to implicate him in the botched raid, though his day-job as an electrician explained the transaction perfectly well.

His stature in the movement was demonstrated during the release campaign organised to stop his threatened deportation after his arrest and trial. The Glasgow *Anarchist* reported that a crowd of 15,000 attended a meeting in Trafalgar Square in June 1912. Later giving his name to the London anarchist club that met variously in High Holborn and Fitzrovia in the 1950s, Malatesta is sometimes said to have been overshadowed by Kropotkin. The two had met in the 1870s and then worked with each other on-and-off until 1914, when Kropotkin came out in support of the war and Malatesta accused him of forgetting his principles. Max Nettlau, the historian of the nineteenth-century European movement, suggested that Kropotkin stole his thunder and that Malatesta's anarchism was always under-appreciated, even though his writings and political practice were "precise and meticulous," as well as "rational, realistic."

It was well known that Malatesta had given up his inheritance and most of his money, and that he earned his reputation with inspectors at the Yard as "an anarchist of a very dangerous type" from tireless insurrectionary activity. But it was not just his personal virtues or his internationalist commitment that make him a great anarchist. Malatesta was particularly alert to the power of propaganda. He started life as a propagandist by the deed and ended it under house arrest in Mussolini's Italy, the year before Hitler became German Chancellor in 1933. Fascists took the art of state propaganda to new heights of sophistication. But Sidney Street had been an object lesson in public relations, providing a glimpse into the everyday manipulations that were to come with mass-televised and online broadcasting. Malatesta already understood that propaganda was a key part of advocacy and that anarchists should practice it in specific ways to counter corporate and state narratives and promote alternative messages.

PROPAGANDA BY THE DEED

In the nineteenth and early twentieth century, 'propaganda by the deed' was usually adopted either to denote revolutionary actions differentiated from publishing (called 'propaganda by the word'), or to describe a method of revolution. Suffragettes legitimised the first usage, organising around the slogan 'deeds not words.' In anarchist history it is more often associated with the wave of individual acts of violence that reached a peak in Europe in the late 1880s and early 1890s. The second meaning was filled out by leading Chinese and Japanese anarchists, amongst others, who advocated assassination as an effective counter to autocracy. The popular misconception, that propaganda by the deed represents the anarchists' terroristic penchant for killing, stems from the de-contextualised blurring of these usages: the revenge violence that was typically directed against heads of state who sanctioned the torture, repression or execution of anarchists, and the defence of tyrannicide as a spur to social transformation.

The decision to struggle for change by means of propaganda – especially propaganda by the deed – was taken by the Bakuninist Jura Federation in 1877 and it was advanced in critique of the Marxist plan to stand workers' candidates in elections. Malatesta had outlined his understanding of the concept the previous year, contrasting it to gradualism and peaceful activism – an approach to action recommended by a minority of socialists in Italy who he characterised as self-seeking and reactionary. While he avoided treating propaganda by the deed as a doctrine that had a fixed or specific content, he linked propagandistic acts firmly to insurrection. Malatesta's judgement of the political situation in Italy at that time was that anarchists should encourage insurrection because this offered "the most effective and the only means" of re-energising internationalist struggle "without deceiving or corrupting" ordinary people.

Malatesta's 1877 action at Benevento, near Naples, is easily and wrongly mocked as an instance of the chaotic and disastrous character of anarchist insurrection. Betrayed by spies, Malatesta was arrested by government troops while trying to incite rebellion in mountain villages. Social revolution was declared but there was no anarchist uprising; however, by the time he was arrested, some locals had burned tax, property and debt registers. He had successfully incited a propagandistic act that not only symbolised resistance to the injustices of ownership, but also entailed a collective refusal to acknowledge the legitimacy of the apparently natural, regulated order. The experience was fleeting yet Benevento was a lesson in anarchy and grand propaganda.

Reflecting on the action in the 1920s, Malatesta wrote that his insurrectionary strategy "had no probability of success" – he had been part of a small band and they had just wanted to raise public awareness of anarchism; however, he remained steadfast in his view that insurrection was an excellent form of anarchist propaganda. Insurrection was "the most potent factor in the emancipation of the people." It focussed attention on "what the people are capable of wanting." At that time, people had been "unaware of the real reasons for their misery." They had "wanted very little" and so had "achieved very little," too. Wondering what they might want from the next insurrection, Malatesta wrote that "the answer ... depends on our propaganda and what efforts we put into it." Given that Mussolini was preparing to stage the March on Rome, this assessment was undoubtedly optimistic. Nevertheless, Malatesta gave it a realist wrapping.

GOVERNMENT AND ANARCHIST PROPAGANDA

In his essay *Anarchy*, Malatesta declared that the accepted defence of government or "the justiciary State" as the "moderator in ... social struggle and impartial administrator of the public interest" was a lie: "an illusion, a utopia never achieved and never to be realised." Government was always the tool of a faction. Whoever exercised control would use its machinery to advance their own interests, all the while doing their utmost to ensure that their rules and norms were internalised by everybody else. Propaganda was the art of getting others to accept a particular vision of reality and dismiss messages about alternatives as single-shot 'propaganda.' Anarchism's demonisation and criminalisation was one measure of the strength of government propaganda. In Malatesta's pamphlet *Fra Contadini, A Dialogue On Anarchy* the character Bert tells the anarchist George: "Father Anthony, who has studied and reads the newspapers, says you're all mad hooligans, that you don't want to work for a living and that instead of doing the workers any good you're preventing the landlords from doing the best they can for us."

Malatesta's analysis resonated with Edward Bernays' view. Bernays was the guru of public relations who tailored his uncle Freud's teachings about desire to suit the management of emergent democracies. In the opening to his 1928 classic *Propaganda*, Bernays observed that the "conscious and intelligent manipulation of the organised habits and opinions of the masses is an important element in democratic society. Those who manipulate this unseen mechanism of society constitute an invisible government which is the true ruling power of our country." The pithy version of the thesis defined propaganda as "the executive arm of the invisible government."

Anarchist propaganda could be differentiated from government propaganda because it was designed to construct a reality that supported alternative power structures – self-governing anarchy. Still, by Malatesta's reckoning, anarchist propaganda was still propaganda. Anarchists had to understand that the marginalised groups they identified with had little-to-no understanding of anarchist principles and were likely to oppose them. Karl Kautsky, and later Lenin, developed the equivalent position in Marxism. This was the idea that workers were unable to achieve class consciousness spontaneously or by their own efforts. Malatesta of course rejected the vanguardist strategy that Lenin proposed to close the gap between the elite and mass. He also rejected Lenin's tactical distinction between propagandists-as-writers and agitators-as-orators. At the same time, he criticised unnamed anarchists (Kropotkinites?) for devoting too much time to devising road maps for anarchy. Writing a year after Bernays, he argued:

> "The important thing is not the victory of our plans, our projects, our utopias, which in any case need the confirmation of experience and can be ... developed and adapted to the real moral and material conditions of the age and place. What matters most is that the people ... lose their sheeplike instincts and habits which thousands of years of slavery have instilled in them, and learn to think and act freely. And it is to this great work of moral liberation that the anarchist must specially dedicate themselves."

Anarchists were not planners but propagandists charged with demonstrating the "uselessness and harmfulness of government, provoking and encouraging, by propaganda and action, all kinds of individual and collective initiatives." Malatesta tasked his comrades with "pushing the people to demand and to seize all the freedom they can and to make themselves responsible for providing their own needs without waiting for orders from any kind of authority."

Anarchist propaganda was "education for freedom." It was about "making people who are accustomed to obedience and passivity consciously aware of their real power and capabilities." But it worked by the same logic as any other form:

> "One must encourage people to do things for themselves, or to think they are doing so by their own initiative and inspiration even when in fact their actions have been suggested by others, just as the good school teacher when he sets a problem his pupil cannot solve immediately, helps him in such a way that the pupil imagines that he has found the solution unaided, thus acquiring courage and confidence in his own abilities."

ANARCHIST PROPAGANDA AND THE CONSTRUCTION OF ALTERNATIVE REALITIES

Acknowledging the potential harms of propaganda was a good way to minimise or avoid them. If propaganda could not always be generated from below and was usually delivered from without, Malatesta's approach underscored a number of anarchist principles: show, don't tell; stand with, not for; expose, don't conceal.

There were no limits on the design of propagandistic acts, except the contexts within which anarchists operated. Malatesta appreciated that it was not always possible for activists to operate openly and that there were "circumstances and actions which demand secrecy"; however, as a general rule, he believed that it was better to "act in the full light of day" rather than covertly or conspiratorially. The "best way to obtain a freedom," he argued, is to take it "facing necessary risks." Propaganda typically involved assertion: "very often a freedom is lost, through one's own fault, either through not exercising it or using it timidly, giving the impression that one has not the right to be doing what one is doing."

There was an ethics to anarchist propaganda, too. This undergirded the distinction between anarchist and government propaganda and differentiated genuinely propagandistic acts from erratic, anarchistic attacks. Anarchist propagandists may choose the same delivery methods as non-anarchists but they had to know their audiences to communicate effectively with them and ensure the clarity of the messages; they had to forge close relationships with the disadvantaged:

> "Isolated, sporadic propaganda which is often a way of easing a troubled conscience or is simply an outlet for someone who has a passion for argument, serves little or no purpose. In the conditions of unawareness and misery in which the masses live, and with so many forces against us, such propaganda is forgotten

and lost before its effect can grow and bear fruit. The soil is too ungrateful for seeds sown haphazardly to germinate and make roots."

Malatesta's rejection of anarchist individualism sprang from this concern. Individualism meant gestural politics. Countering government propaganda required "continuity of effort, patience, coordination and adaptability to different surroundings and circumstances" – clear-sightedness, organisation and flexibility.

RUTH KINNA

––––––––––

Ruth Kinna is a professor of Political Theory at Loughborough University, working in the Department of Politics, History and International Relations where she specialises in political philosophy. Since 2007 she has been the editor of the journal Anarchist Studies.

CLIFFORD HARPER

––––––––––

Clifford Harper is a worker, illustrator, and militant anarchist. He has worked for many radical and alternative publications, the international anarchist movement and almost all of the UK national newspapers.

DOG SECTION PRESS

————

Dog Section Press is a not-for-profit publisher and distributor of seditious literature, and a registered worker-owned cooperative.

ACTIVE DISTRIBUTION PUBLISHING

————

Active Distribution Publishing continues the publishing side of Active Distribution, a DIY not-for-profit venture dedicated to spreading the anarchist word as cheaply as possible since 1989.

ACTIVE DISTRIBUTION